D1214563

Presented to

---

from

LIVING THE
66 BOOKS OF THE BIBLE

P.O. Box 3838
San Diego, CA 92163

Edited by Robert J. Morgan.
Unless indicated otherwise, Scripture verses quoted are from the New King James Version.

Printed in China.

LIVING THE

66 BOOKS OF THE BIBLE

DAVID JEREMIAH

Table of Contents

Introduction 11

OLD TESTAMENT

Genesis 16
Exodus 20
Leviticus 24
Numbers 28
Deuteronomy 32
Joshua 36
Judges 40
Ruth 44
1 Samuel 48
2 Samuel 52
1 Kings 56
2 Kings 60
1 Chronicles 64
2 Chronicles 68
Ezra 72
Nehemiah 76
Esther 80
Job 84
Psalms 88

Proverbs 92
Ecclesiastes 96
Song of Solomon 100
Isaiah 104
Jeremiah 108
Lamentations 112
Ezekiel 116
Daniel 120
Hosea 124
Joel 128
Amos 132
Obadiah 136
Jonah 140
Micah 144
Nahum 148
Habakkuk 152
Zephaniah 156
Haggai 160
Zechariah 164
Malachi 168

NEW TESTAMENT

Matthew 174
Mark 178
Luke 182

John 186
Acts 190
Romans 194
1 Corinthians 198
2 Corinthians 202
Galatians 206
Ephesians 210
Philippians 214
Colossians 218
1 Thessalonians 222
2 Thessalonians 226
1 Timothy 230
2 Timothy 234
Titus 238
Philemon 242
Hebrews 246
James 250
1 Peter 254
2 Peter 258
1 John 262
2 John 266
3 John 270
Jude 274
Revelation 278

Additional Resources 283

Introduction

Do you know anyone who still uses a sewing machine? Imagine cutting out the pages of the Bible and sewing them together to make a suit for you or a dress or a coat for the winter. What if all our clothes were stitched together from paper cut from a Bible?

That's what I want to suggest in this book.

We need to wear the Scripture, to be clothed with the teachings of Christ and to be clad in the Word of Life. When people see us, may they see walking Bibles!

I've never relished Bible study more than now. It seems the older we become, the more we love God's Word. If you were to see me at my desk at home, you'd see an open Bible with study resources and commentaries opened left and right. My notepads are never far from my pen.

But there's always a danger that Bible study will fail to translate into biblical living. It's one thing to understand the 66 books of the Bible. It's another thing to live them, to put them into practice, and to be doers of the Word.

In this book, I've taken the 66 books of Scripture—Genesis to Revelation—and sought to show their implications for daily life. Each segment has an overview of the book at hand

and its practical message, along with its stated theme, a suggested challenge, a key verse, and a prayer.

And my prayer?

That we would both *learn* and *live the* Word of God, for our own joy and for the benefit of those who need so badly to see it.

Nothing can touch this world so deeply as a walking Bible!

Why not let it be you!

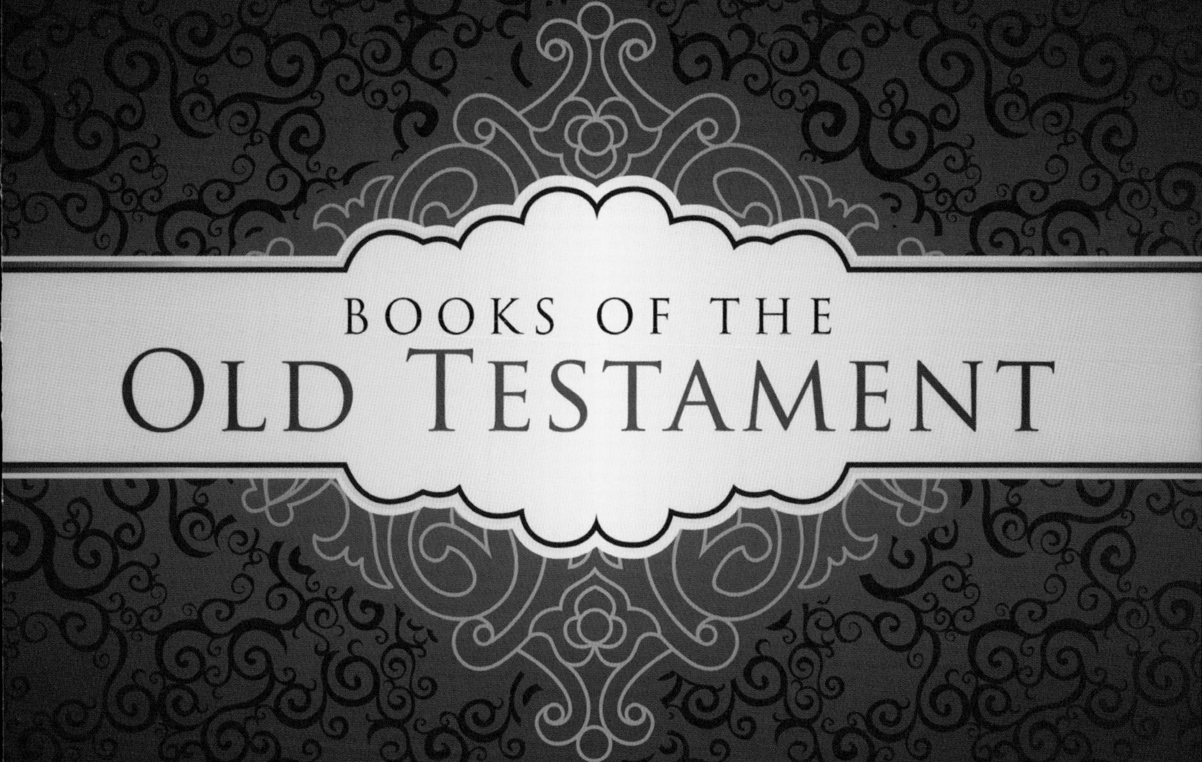
BOOKS OF THE
OLD TESTAMENT

GENESIS

ife is full of new beginnings. Every morning begins a new day; every Sunday brings a new week; every January starts a new year. Our Lord is the God of new beginnings, and that's the theme of Genesis. The first words of the Bible are, "In the beginning God" (Genesis 1:1).

The very word *Genesis* is related to genes and genetics—the issue of origins and beginnings.

Everyone who decided to follow the Lord in Genesis needed a new beginning at some point, and often at many points in their lives. Think of Adam and Eve after they were driven from the Garden of Eden (3:24); Noah, after the flood (9:1); Abraham, who left his home in Ur (12:1); Jacob, whose life was one disaster after another until the Lord wrestled with him and blessed him (32:2-28). Don't forget Joseph who had a new beginning in Egypt, where God had sent him as a prisoner to become a prince (41:41).

Our Lord is eager to provide as many new beginnings as we need.

Without that truth, life is dark and dangerous. But our eternal Creator stretches His watchful grace over every second of every day. Even when the enemy presses us, God's sovereignty will prevail. His plan for us will succeed.

In Genesis 22:14, God is called by the title: "The Lord Will Provide" (Jehovah Jireh). If you need a new beginning, He is ready with fresh provision and encouragement.

KEY THEME:

Remember that no matter what life brings or how evil intrudes, our Creator has a plan, His sovereignty cannot be thwarted, and His plan is right on schedule.

KEY CHALLENGE:

Think of every morning as a new opportunity to trust the Lord with all your burdens and cares; begin each day with a renewed commitment to love and serve Him with all your heart.

KEY VERSE:

"I will bless you...and you shall be a blessing" (Genesis 12:2).

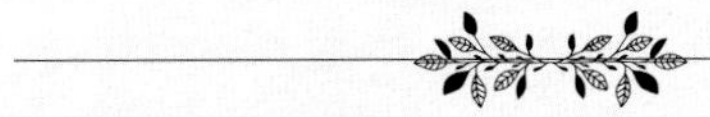

KEY PRAYER:

Lord, thank You that in all things I can trust You to lead and guide me—for You are always with me—giving me a new beginning when needed, for Your plan for me is good.

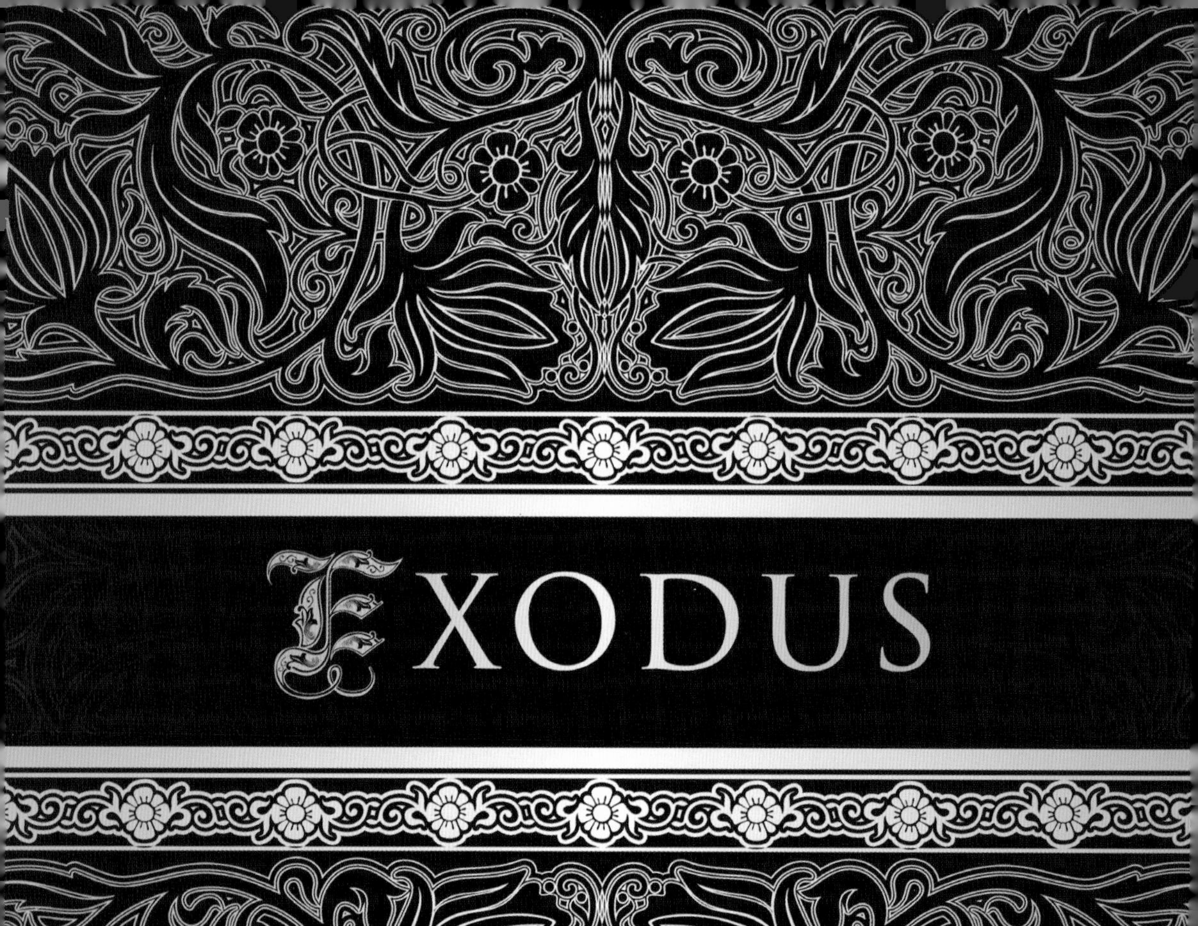

EXODUS

xodus is an epic story of God's mighty deliverance in breaking the power of ancient Egypt. He rebuked its gods, thwarted its Pharaoh, and delivered His people. As the book opens, the nation of Israel—descendants of Abraham—are enslaved in Egypt. God sent Moses with a message to Pharoah, "Thus says the Lord God of Israel: 'Let My people go'" (Exodus 5:1). The Lord also sent a series of plagues to ravage Egypt, then He delivered His people through the parted waters of the Red Sea (chapter 14). At Mount Sinai, He told them how to live. The last part of the book describes the tabernacle—where the "glory of the Lord filled the tabernacle" (40:34) and He dwelt among His people (40:38).

Just like the Israelites, each of us has problems we cannot solve in our own strength or by our own resources. We need the God of Israel! He tells us to give Him our fears and to receive His strengthening grace. He alone can part the waters and do things that are impossible for us.

You can trust Him with any pharaoh-sized problem you have. Turn the Red Sea experience you're facing over to Him by faith, and then be still, trust Him, wait on Him, and see what He will do!

Remember, He wants your obedience, and He also longs to dwell within you and around you. As He hovered above the children of Israel as a cloud by day and fire by night, so He will hover over you all the days of your life. Be aware of His presence and power!

KEY THEME:

Just as God delivered His people from slavery to freedom, He is present in your life today—leading, delivering, and providing for your needs. God is with you!

KEY CHALLENGE:

Thank God for His presence and protection every day, giving your concerns, whether great or small, into His loving care.

KEY VERSE:

"Do not be afraid. Stand still, and see the salvation of the Lord, which He will accomplish for you today" (Exodus 14:13).

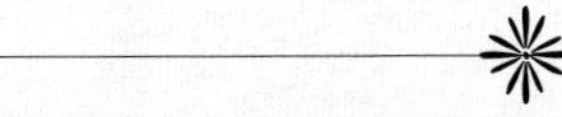

KEY PRAYER:

Lord, thank You for the assurance that You are with me in my time of trouble. Strengthen me to stand firm and wait patiently as I wait for Your deliverance.

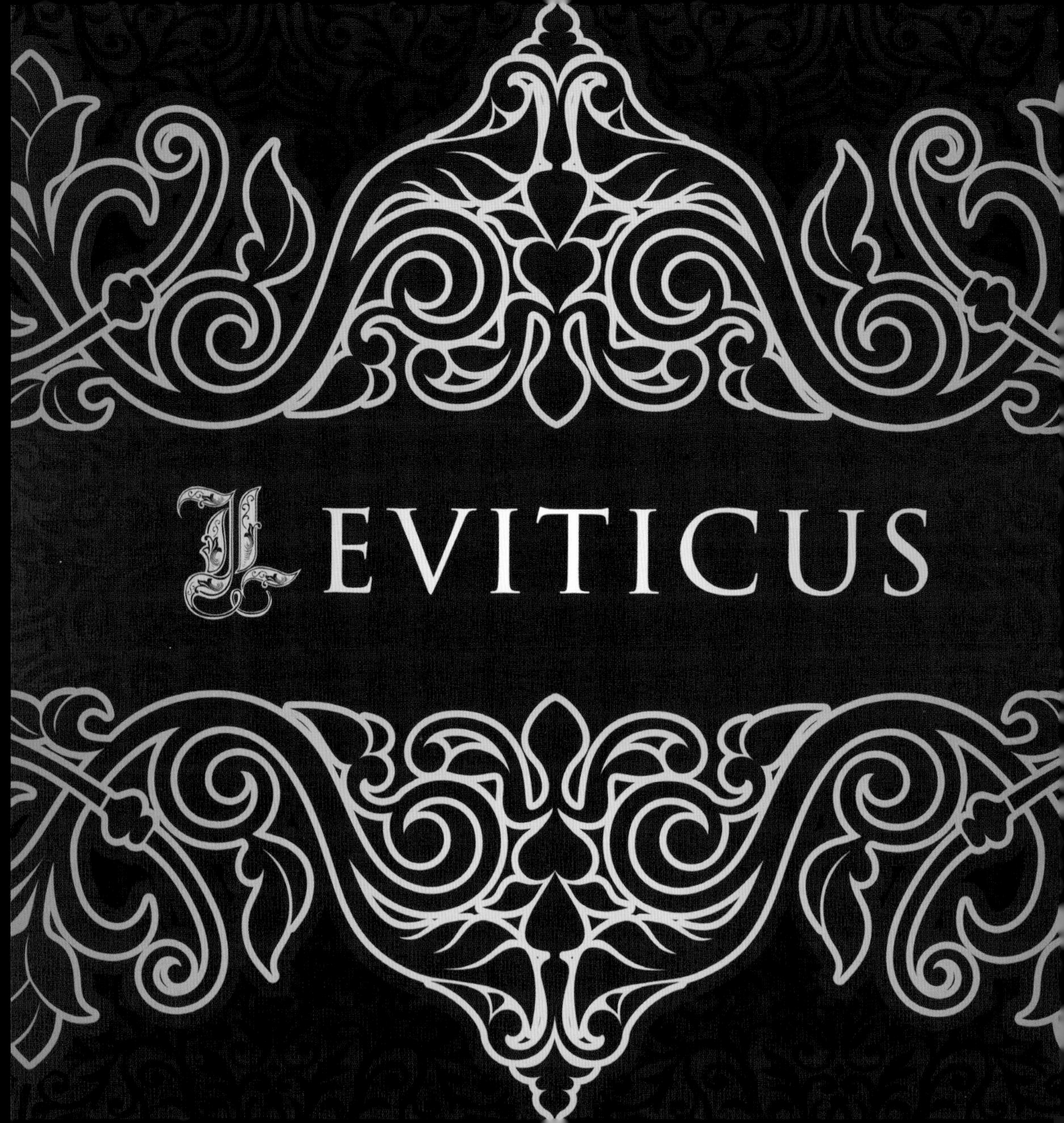

LEVITICUS

oliness! That's the message of Leviticus, which is a record of the instructions God gave the Israelites at Mount Sinai (Leviticus 1:1). When we speak of God's holiness, it refers to His absolute purity and sinless essence. We are not like that, so coming into God's presence is impossible without His provision of grace. For Israel, that involved a system of offerings (chapters 1–7) and a priesthood (chapters 8–17)—both of which pointed toward the ministry of Christ. The last part of Leviticus told Israel how to live in a holy manner (chapters 18–27).

Leviticus teaches us to approach a Holy God only through the sacrifice and ministry of Jesus, our great High Priest (Hebrews 2:17). When we receive God's grace through Christ, we long to live a life of growing personal holiness. God's children reflect His character, and we must diligently ask Him to make us increasingly like Christ.

Is there an area of your life that lapses into an unholy state? The key to godliness is learning to detect sin in your life, confess it earnestly, and avoid it relentlessly. We can only do that through the Holy Spirit. His very title—*Holy Spirit*—reflects the theme of Leviticus. As He lives and moves within us, His major aim is perfecting holiness in us so we'll be pleasing to our Heavenly Father.

Remember Leviticus 20:26 as a personal challenge: "And you shall be holy to Me, for I the Lord am holy, and have separated you from the peoples, that you should be Mine."

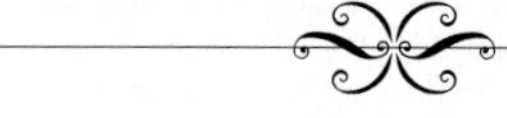

KEY THEME:

Whenever we sin, we should confess it promptly, consecrate ourselves anew, and remain committed to personal holiness.

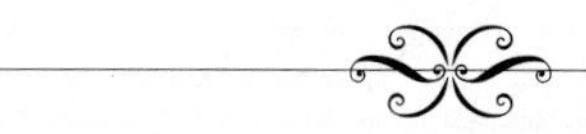

KEY CHALLENGE:

Begin the process of identifying and then removing unhealthy habits in your life so that you reflect the holiness of God.

KEY VERSE:

"Consecrate yourselves therefore, and be holy, for I am the Lord your God" (Leviticus 20:7).

KEY PRAYER:

Father, purify my heart, forgive me of my sin, and help me to live a life that reflects Your holiness to the world around me.

NUMBERS

eware to whom you listen!

The book of Numbers begins at Mount Sinai (Numbers 1–10), follows the Israelites as they prepare to enter the Promised Land (Numbers 11–12), and records their terrible decision to listen to the ten doubtful spies instead of the two, Joshua and Caleb, who encouraged them to possess the land (Numbers 13).

Caleb quieted the people saying, “Let us go up at once and take possession, for we are well able to overcome it” (Numbers 13:30). But the masses were afraid and didn’t trust God to keep His promise to go with them to give them the land. The last part of the book (Numbers 14–36) tells of their forty years of wandering in exile because of their unbelief.

The Lord has promised to bless you and give you an appointed future in this life and an eternity with Him. The blessing used by the priests for Israel is for us too—"The Lord bless you and keep you; the Lord make His face shine upon you, and be gracious to you; the Lord lift up His countenance upon you, and give you peace" (Numbers 6:24-26).

How important to take those words as our own, relying on God to fulfill them even when we face challenges and heartache. As God's children, we should have a positive attitude of victory and be unafraid to venture forward wherever He leads—for He will do as He says.

Let's listen, most of all, to Him!

KEY THEME:

Trust God's Word even when challenges appear, for His promises are unchanging and undeniable.

KEY CHALLENGE:

Determine to trust God and claim His promise to bless you, keep you, smile upon you, and give you peace.

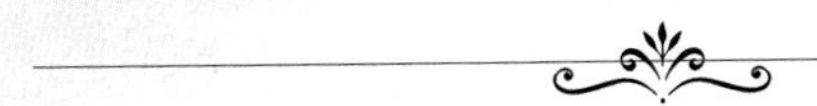

KEY VERSE:

"The Lord bless you and keep you; the Lord make His face shine upon you, and be gracious to you; the Lord lift up His countenance upon you, and give you peace" (Numbers 6:24-26).

KEY PRAYER:

Heavenly Father, help me to keep my eyes on You, to trust in Your timing, and to remember that You always keep Your promises!

DEUTERONOMY

efore Moses passed the reigns of leadership to Joshua, he had the opportunity once again to explain the Word of God to the Israelites—warning against idolatry, to honor the Ten Commandments, to remember the blessing of obedience, the importance of not forgetting the Lord, and more. Deuteronomy is, in essence, a series of messages given to the younger generation of Israelites by Moses, just before he relinquished leadership and died. In chapters 1 through 4, he reviewed the wanderings of the Israelites. In chapters 5 through 26, he told Israel how to live; and in chapters 27 through 34, he told them how to go onward.

Throughout the book is a resounding theme—to remember and share all these things with your children and grandchildren. Deuteronomy 4:10 says, "Gather the people to Me, and I will let them hear My words...that they may teach their children." Moses told them to keep God's words on their hearts and "teach them diligently to your children...when you sit in your house, when you walk by the way, when you lie down, and when you rise up" (Deuteronomy 6:7).

Deuteronomy 29:29 says, "Those things which are revealed belong to us and to our children forever, that we may do all the words of this law."

We don't have to be well-read theologians to share what we've learned in the Bible with a child or other loved one. The most powerful words we can say are: "Let me tell you about the verse God showed me today in His Word. May I encourage you with this Scripture today?"

Make it a deliberate pattern to naturally and spontaneously share the good things God is showing you day by day.

KEY THEME:

Share God's Truth with the generations to follow so that the Word of the Lord is not forgotten.

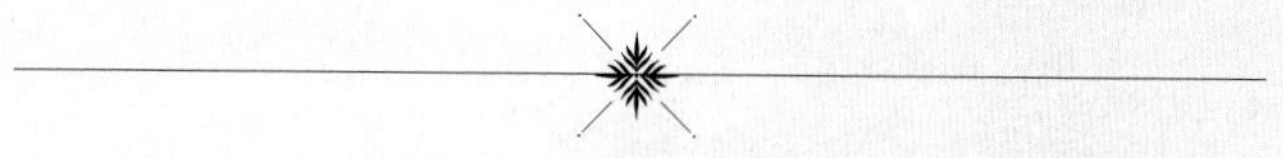

KEY CHALLENGE:

Find ways to share the Word of God
with someone you know!

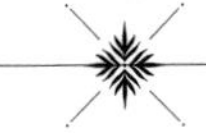

KEY VERSE:

"You shall teach them diligently to your children, and shall talk of them when you sit in your house, when you walk by the way, when you lie down, and when you rise up" (Deuteronomy 6:7).

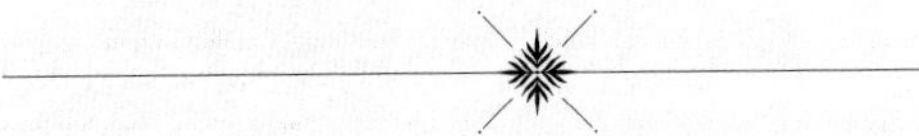

KEY PRAYER:

Lord, give me the boldness to share Your Truth with my family—especially those who don't know You as their Savior.

JOSHUA

fter the death of Moses, God commissioned Joshua to lead the Israelites across the Jordan River into the land promised to Abraham's descendants. The book of Joshua tells the story of the possession and division of the land by the tribes of Israel. The first half of the book (chapters 1–12) tells how Israel took possession of the Promised Land; and the last half (chapters 13–24) describes how the various tribes settled into their allotted portions.

At the end of the book, Joshua gave his farewell address. He reminded the Israelites of God's guidance and power, telling them, "Behold, this day I am going the way of all the earth. And you know in all your hearts and in all your souls that not one thing has failed of all the good things which the Lord your God spoke concerning you" (Joshua 23:14).

He warned them against reverting to the gods of Egypt or adopting the gods of the people whom they had dispossessed, and he proclaimed with holy audacity: "But as for me and my house, we will serve the Lord" (Joshua 24:15).

We're living in an age of many gods, many philosophies, many temptations. We can't control the culture around us, but we can—and we must—say: "But as for me and my house, we will serve the Lord."

Not one good thing has failed in all the Lord has promised you. Let nothing stop you from serving the Lord all your days with all your heart.

KEY THEME:

Claim His promises! God is faithful; choose this day to serve the Lord.

KEY CHALLENGE:

Live out Joshua 24:15 by putting biblical principles into practice that guide you at home and in your community!

KEY VERSE:

"Choose for yourselves this day whom you will serve.... But as for me and my house, we will serve the Lord" (Joshua 24:15).

KEY PRAYER:

Lord, I choose this day to serve You.
May I put You first in every area of my life so that the world will see You in me.

JUDGES

ou've heard of a "vicious cycle." That's the story of all 21 chapters of Judges. After the death of Joshua, no national leader emerged. The tribes began doing what was right in their own eyes (Judges 17:6), and a recurring pattern developed. When the people yielded to temptation and ceased following the Lord, their enemies attacked and ravaged them. Then the Israelites repented and turned back to God. The Lord raised up leaders like Deborah, Gideon, Jair, and Samson to give them victory. But eventually the people relapsed into complacency and the entire cycle was repeated.

Judges is full of stories, some of them tragic and sickening. These are vivid warnings to us. The "vicious cycle" still whirls around us, and we must guard against ease and complacency. The Christian life is not static. We're either drawing closer to the Lord each day, or we're slipping further from Him.

Perhaps the most encouraging verse in Judges was spoken to Gideon, when the Angel of the Lord told him, “The Lord is with you, you mighty man of valor!” (Judges 6:12) Gideon didn’t feel that way; he felt helpless and insignificant. But the Lord was with him and used him to save Israel from her enemies.

The Lord is with you too, and He knows how greatly you can serve Him. Don’t allow lapses, carelessness, small sins, large faults, or busyness to distract you from your devotion to Him. Draw ever closer to Him. Let every day with Jesus be better than the one before.

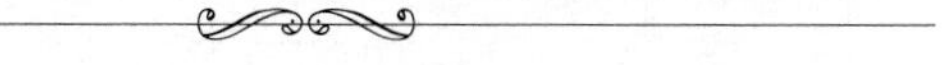

KEY THEME:

We must break the cycle of apathy, sin, ruin, defeat, and despair with the power of lasting repentance and revival.

KEY CHALLENGE:

Examine yourself to see if you're closer to the Lord today than you were yesterday. Reject the cycle of complacency and regret and remember that as you draw near to Him, He will draw near to you.

KEY VERSE:

"And when the Lord raised up judges for them, the Lord was with the judge and delivered them out of the hand of their enemies.... And it came to pass, when the judge was dead, that they reverted and behaved more corruptly than their fathers" (Judges 2:18-19).

KEY PRAYER:

Father, help me to resist temptation and to seek You with my whole heart—remembering nothing will change in my life unless my heart changes.

RUTH

ollowing the tragic stories in Judges, we're ready for a ray of sunlight. The book of Ruth is a two-fold story. It's about Naomi, whose life became bitter after fleeing to Moab. It's also about her widowed daughter-in-law, Ruth, who became a follower of the God of Israel, the wife of Boaz, and the mother of Obed, who became the grandfather of King David.

The book of Ruth begins in Bethlehem, moves to Moab, then shifts back to Bethlehem—first in the fields, then on the threshing floor of Boaz, then at the town gate. The drama is redemptive, for it tells how God took an embittered older woman and a bereaved younger one and provided for them a lasting inheritance through a "close relative" or a "kinsman redeemer."

The Lord Jesus Christ—humanly speaking, a descendant of Ruth—is our close relative and Kinsman Redeemer. He can take our bitterness and bereavement, touch it with Calvary's grace, and bring forth blessings and a legacy of hope. The same lesson is in Joel 2:25, when the Lord said, "So I will restore to you the years that the swarming locust has eaten." Nehemiah 13:2 makes the same point: "However, our God turned the curse into a blessing."

In times of suffering and lingering sadness based upon past hardships, kneel and give your pain to God. Naomi wanted to change her name to "Mara," meaning *bitter[ness]* (Ruth 1:20), but the Lord banished her bitterness and brought blessing into her life as she steadfastly trusted Him.

He will do the same for you!

KEY THEME:

Trust in the God who redeems the hardships of our past, blesses us now, and provides for our future.

KEY CHALLENGE:

When adversity or sadness overwhelm you, reject the tendency to become bitter. Find a place and time to pray, asking and expecting God to turn your sorrow into joy in His perfect time.

KEY VERSE:

"Blessed be the Lord, who has not left you this day without a close relative; and may his name be famous in Israel!" (Ruth 4:14)

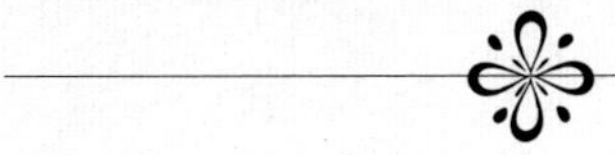

KEY PRAYER:

Thank You, Lord, for bringing beauty from ashes in my life and for Your unfailing love to me, my Kinsman Redeemer.

I SAMUEL

ave you ever changed your initial impression of someone after getting to know them? Because we're not born with X-ray vision, we base our opinions on what we can see. Sometimes we take an instant dislike to people because of their mannerisms, style of dress, momentary expressions, or stated opinions. God sees through all those externals in one glance, for He X-rays the heart.

That's one of the main lessons of 1 Samuel, which tells about three leaders—Samuel (chapters 1–8), Saul (chapters 9–15), and David (chapters 16–31). The stories of the three overlap but the chapter divisions clearly show how the storyline changes from one to the other—Samuel, the seasoned leader; Saul, the foolish one; and David, the emerging one.

Despite his wisdom, Samuel missed seeing David's potential. He was the youngest of Jesse's sons, not as impressive as his older, taller siblings with their impressive faces. Yet God saw in young David “a man after His own heart” (1 Samuel 13:14).

There are two lessons for us in this. First, we shouldn’t be overly concerned about how impressive we appear to others. Our beauty should not be primarily outward, but “the hidden person of the heart” (1 Peter 3:3-4). Second, we ought to be cautious in jumping to conclusions about others. Ask God to give you a discerning mind so you can better see with God’s eyesight. The person you least like may be the one God wants you to most love.

KEY THEME:

Don’t judge by first impressions, for God doesn’t look at people as we do. We look at the external appearance, but the Lord looks at the heart.

KEY CHALLENGE:

As you prepare for your day each morning, ask the Lord to give you a cheerful spirit and a smile to begin your day—be ready and willing to accept others as God has accepted you.

KEY VERSE:

"But the Lord said to Samuel, 'Do not look at his appearance or at his physical stature, because I have refused him. For the Lord does not see as man sees; for man looks at the outward appearance, but the Lord looks at the heart'" (1 Samuel 16:7).

KEY PRAYER:

Dear God, please help me see others through Your eyes and not as the world sees them. I praise You for forgiving and accepting me—my Lord and the Rock of my salvation.

II SAMUEL

he book of 2 Samuel can be summed up in one word: David. It's the story of his forty-year reign over Judah and Israel. The first ten chapters tell us how he built his kingdom. The next ten tell us, sadly, how he wrecked his life. Yet God in His mercy led David to contrition, repentance, and restoration, making him the greatest Israelite king in the Bible and the great composer of many of the Psalms of the Old Testament.

Like David, we aren't perfect. May the Lord keep us from sin, especially the kinds of sins that wreck our reputations and bring reproach on His Kingdom! But only in heaven will there be a sinless environment for sinless people. Until then, we must constantly and continually live under the reign and rule of Jesus Christ, the Son of David, and the King of Righteousness.

Perhaps the key moment in 2 Samuel occurred in chapter 7, when God made a covenant with David to "set up your seed after you" and to "establish his kingdom" (verse 12). The Lord was talking about Solomon but pointing to someone greater than Solomon. Verse 16 says, "And your house and your kingdom shall be established forever before you. Your throne shall be established forever."

Our Lord Jesus Christ is eternal and of His Kingdom there will be no end. Let us honor Him, yield to Him, and serve Him without wavering. Let's say: "O worship the King, all glorious above, and gratefully sing His power and His love."[1]

KEY THEME:

Acknowledge God's kingship in every area of life.

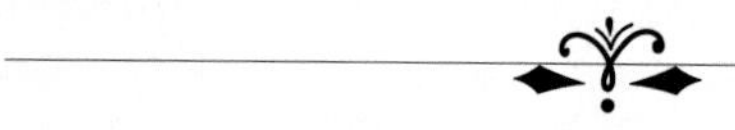

KEY CHALLENGE:

When you pray, pray in the Name of King Jesus! Make it a practice to remember that He is our sovereign Lord and submit to His authority in your life.

KEY VERSE:

"Therefore You are great, O Lord God. For there is none like You, nor is there any God besides You, according to all that we have heard with our ears" (2 Samuel 7:22).

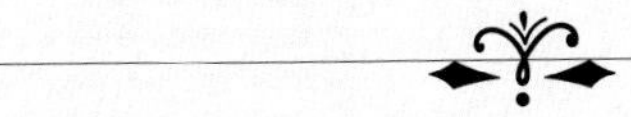

KEY PRAYER:

Lord, please reign as my sovereign King in every area of my life. Help me to submit to Your authority and to reject the innate desire to have my own way.

[1] Robert Grant, "O Worship the King All Glorious Above," 1833.

I KINGS

he book of 1 Kings breaks into two parts. The first eleven chapters are about Solomon, and the last eleven are about the kings who followed him, both in the South and the North in the land of Israel. Under Solomon, the nation reached its golden age. The nation benefitted from his wisdom, and people traveled far and wide to hear his teachings. For years, his kingdom was at peace. The wealth of nations flowed into Jerusalem.

Solomon's wisdom exceeded a high IQ. It was a God-given wisdom in response to the request Solomon made as a young man. He asked God to give him an understanding heart to know good and evil. The Lord made the same offer to us in James 1:5: "If any of you lacks wisdom, let him ask of God, who gives to all liberally and without reproach, and it will be given to him."

We can be wiser than Solomon because we serve a King greater than Solomon. Though Solomon's wisdom brought times of prosperity to Jerusalem, it also brought peril to Solomon's own heart. He became too self-aware, too sensual, too desensitized to the Lord's voice.

It's important to pray each day for needed wisdom; God teaches us morning by morning. We learn much in times of peril, but we also need insight for navigating prosperity, lest we make a shipwreck of our faith. Our prayer should be: "Lord, grant me all the needed wisdom day by day. May I speak wisely at all times and walk wisely in all ways."

KEY THEME:

Let's be as cautious in times of prosperity as we are in times of peril, lest we relax our guard and allow our spiritual passion to grow lukewarm.

KEY CHALLENGE:

When facing decisive moments, ask God for discernment and wisdom to know what to do. Make it a practice to trust Him even when you cannot understand His leading, for our understanding is imperfect, but He is wise in all His ways.

KEY VERSE:

"Therefore give to Your servant an understanding heart to judge Your people, that I may discern between good and evil. For who is able to judge this great people of Yours?" (1 Kings 3:9)

KEY PRAYER:

God, give me a renewed passion for Your Word and a heart to follow You and to obey Your commands.

II KINGS

ots of kings! That's the story of this book, which covers the history of the Jews after Solomon. The nation divided into two kingdoms. The Northern Kingdom began serving foreign gods from the beginning, and it was destroyed by Assyria in 722 B.C. The Southern Kingdom had periods of revival, but fell to the Babylonians in 586 B.C. Most of the kings were corrupt, but there were some heroes, not only among the monarchs but among the prophets.

Perhaps the most exciting stories involve Elijah and Elisha, and we can learn rich spiritual lessons from their lives. In 2 Kings 6, the King of Syria sent his army to Dothan to trap and destroy Elisha. Troops surrounded the city by night. The next morning, Elisha's servant realized what was happening and cried out, "Alas!" But Elisha said, "Do not fear, for those who are with us are more than those who are with them" (verses 15-16). The Lord opened the servant's eyes to see the invisible armies of the heavenly host, who were there to protect God's servants.

Whenever you see the words “Do not fear” in the Bible, pay attention. In this case, fear was unfounded because of angelic helpers. The same help is afforded to us more times than we know. Psalm 34:7 says, “The angel of the Lord encamps all around those who fear Him.” And Psalm 91:11 says, “He shall give His angels charge over you, to keep you in all your ways.”

When you’re walking with the Lord, you needn’t fear. You’re in good hands!

KEY THEME:

We, like Elijah, should live with confidence in chaotic times, for we are protected by the invisible armies of the Lord of hosts.

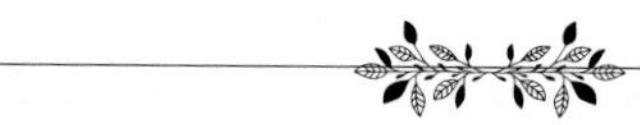

KEY CHALLENGE:

When you are tempted to succumb to fear, claim this promise: "I have angelic helpers who are always with me!"

KEY VERSE:

"And Elisha prayed, and said, 'Lord, I pray, open his eyes that he may see.' Then the Lord opened the eyes of the young man, and he saw. And behold, the mountain was full of horses and chariots of fire all around Elisha" (2 Kings 6:17).

KEY PRAYER:

Heavenly Father, help me to live confidently, knowing You are protecting and guiding me through every situation I encounter in life.

I CHRONICLES

his is a very encouraging book. Though the first nine chapters are genealogies, there are some rich surprises there (see 1 Chronicles 4:10). Chapter 10 gives a brief word about King Saul, and the rest of the book is about the way God led, blessed, and used David as the King of Israel. It also tells us of David's dream to build a vast temple to the Lord. Though Solomon built the temple, it was David who developed the plans and raised the money. It was his last great endeavor.

In 1 Chronicles 28, David assembled all the leaders of Israel to Jerusalem to listen as he charged Solomon with the construction of this building, which would be the dwelling place of the Lord. David told his son, "Be strong and of good courage, and do it; do not fear nor be dismayed, for the Lord God—my God—will be with you. He will not leave you nor forsake you, until you have finished all the work for the service of the house of the Lord" (verse 20).

The Lord has work for you too. He searches our hearts, knows our thoughts, and draws us to Himself. He ordains our daily tasks, and He uses us in ways we don't even understand. In whatever you do, be strong and of good courage. Do as the Lord directs you. Don't be afraid. He will be with you and will not forsake you until the work is finished—and not even then!

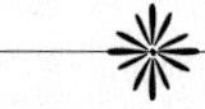

KEY THEME:

Worship the Lord as King and labor joyfully in the service of His work.

KEY CHALLENGE:

Search for ways to serve the Lord daily in the work He has planned for you.

KEY VERSE:

"Know the God of your father, and serve Him with a loyal heart and with a willing mind; for the Lord searches all hearts and understands all the intent of the thoughts" (1 Chronicles 28:9).

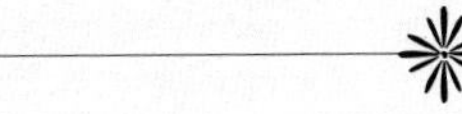

KEY PRAYER:

Lord, thank You for the privilege of serving You! May I serve You with a joyful heart each day.

II CHRONICLES

he word *temple* occurs nearly fifty times in 2 Chronicles, and for good reason. The entire book revolves around God dwelling among His people. When Solomon built the temple, the glory of the Lord filled it, and God's presence indwelled the Holy of Holies. When we read about the fire coming down and filling the sanctuary, it reminds us of how the Holy Spirit later descended on the Day of Pentecost, filling each believer (Acts 2:1-4). The apostle Paul later told us: "Or do you not know that your body is the temple of the Holy Spirit who is in you, whom you have from God, and you are not your own?" (1 Corinthians 6:19)

Think of it! How glorious!

The same presence that resided in the heart of Solomon's Jerusalem has a different address now. He resides within you and me. In these Last Days, we are His temple, His home.

What happens in the temple? Glorious worship. The blowing of trumpets. The singing of praises. The joy of fellowship with the Almighty. The proclamation of the Good News that God lives among us.

We have an obligation to keep our bodies and spirits as healthy as possible, and to use them as wisely as we can. We're to be a *holy* temple. No medical scan will detect Him, but the Holy Spirit is within your body as truly as He dwelt within Solomon's temple.

We are to praise Him and to exalt His name together!

KEY THEME:

Glorify God in the temple where He resides—in your body and spirit. Be faithful in joyful worship.

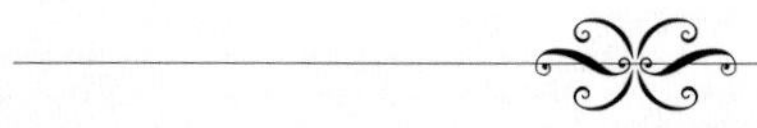

KEY CHALLENGE:

Let your life be a habitation of praise. Praise Him throughout your day in song, in prayer, and in your conversation.

KEY VERSE:

"When Solomon had finished praying, fire came down from heaven and consumed the burnt offering...and the glory of the Lord filled the temple" (2 Chronicles 7:1).

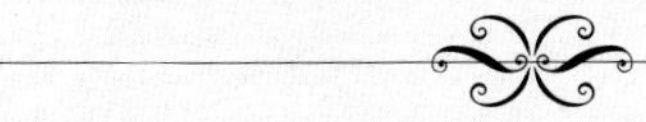

KEY PRAYER:

Father, may my life glorify You—in my body and my spirit—where Your Holy Spirit resides within me.

EZRA

o understand the book of Ezra, it's important to know it tells two stories. The first six chapters describe the first group of exiles who came from Babylon to rebuild the temple and restore the city of Jerusalem. There follows a gap of nearly sixty years, and chapters 7 through 10 speak of the second group of exiles who returned under the leadership of Ezra to restore solid Bible teaching to Israel in its own homeland.

The rebuilding of the temple in the first part of the book involved hard labor. When the exiles arrived in Jerusalem, the temple mount was nothing but ruins covered with vines and weeds, a haunt for wild dogs and jackals. Slowly but surely, the workers cleared away the debris. The first thing they did was restore the altar that had stood before the temple, allowing them to again offer sacrifices for sin (Ezra 3:2).

That altar anticipated the cross of Christ, and we can learn something from the story.

How often we need to rebuild something in our lives that has become broken down! We are under construction, and the Lord who has begun a good work in us is determined to complete it (Philippians 1:6). Whenever we need a new beginning or a mid-course correction, we have to kneel at Calvary for fresh grace and renewed zeal.

Fanny Crosby wrote, "Jesus, keep me near the cross, there a precious fountain; free to all, a healing stream, flows from Calv'ry's mountain."[2]

May the cross of Jesus Christ be our glory forever!

KEY THEME:

In rebuilding anything, we must start with the altar, reestablishing the cross of Jesus Christ as central to our lives and activities.

KEY CHALLENGE:

Stay near the cross of our Lord, watching, waiting, hoping, and trusting in its redemptive power.

KEY VERSE:

"And they sang responsively, praising and giving thanks to the Lord: 'For He is good, for His mercy endures forever toward Israel.' Then all the people shouted with a great shout, when they praised the Lord, because the foundation of the house of the Lord was laid" (Ezra 3:11).

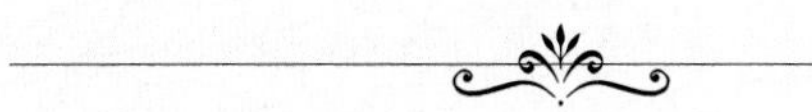

KEY PRAYER:

Heavenly Father, thank You for Your gift of the Gospel. May the gift of salvation through Christ's death on the cross remain central to all I do and say in my life.

[2] Fanny Crosby, "Near the Cross," 1869.

NEHEMIAH

isitors to modern Jerusalem are shown a section of an ancient stone wall that reportedly dates back to Nehemiah. Nehemiah is remembered as one of history's most gifted builders, and the Old Testament book bearing his name is a leadership manual on tackling and finishing projects for the Lord. Nehemiah returned from Persia to rebuild Jerusalem's defensive wall for the protection of God's people. He didn't just organize the rebuilding of the wall. He raised up the city's militia, established the land's financial ethics, guided its temple worship, and labored to bring about spiritual reform.

In chapter 2, Nehemiah went out by night to inspect the city's broken walls, to think about his strategy, and to develop his plan. He told no one until he was sure of God's intentions. Then he rallied the people and led the project.

The Lord wants to give all of us a vision of what He wants us to do. We're all leaders in some way, and God has placed us on earth to build some walls or repair some breaches. What is His vision for your life? What work can you do? What breach can you heal? Ask God to show you, then study the needs around you and prayerfully develop your vision.

Nehemiah knew the work wasn't simply in his hands. He felt "the good hand of my God upon me" (Nehemiah 2:8). The Lord's good hand will be on you too as you fulfill the personal vision He gives you.

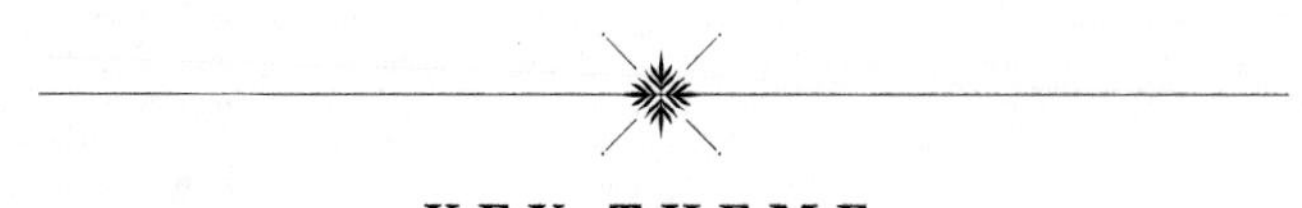

KEY THEME:

All of us can become better leaders by studying the life and methods of Nehemiah.

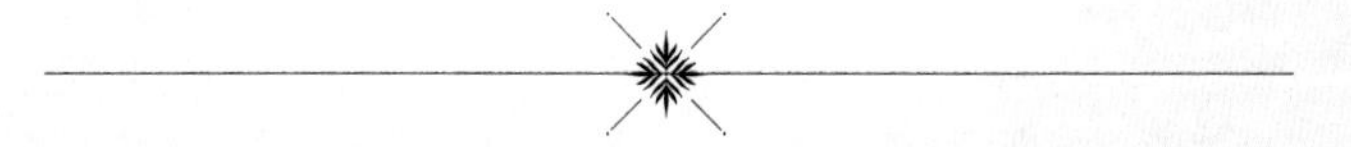

KEY CHALLENGE:

Find a need in the life of someone you know and determine how you can be of help to them. That's a good place to start building a personal vision.

KEY VERSE:

"Then I said to them, 'You see the distress that we are in.... Come and let us build the wall of Jerusalem....' And I told them of the hand of my God which had been good upon me.... So they said, 'Let us rise up and build.' Then they set their hands to this good work" (Nehemiah 2:17-18).

KEY PRAYER:

Lord, thank You for the men and women in Scripture whose example I can follow in my walk of faith.

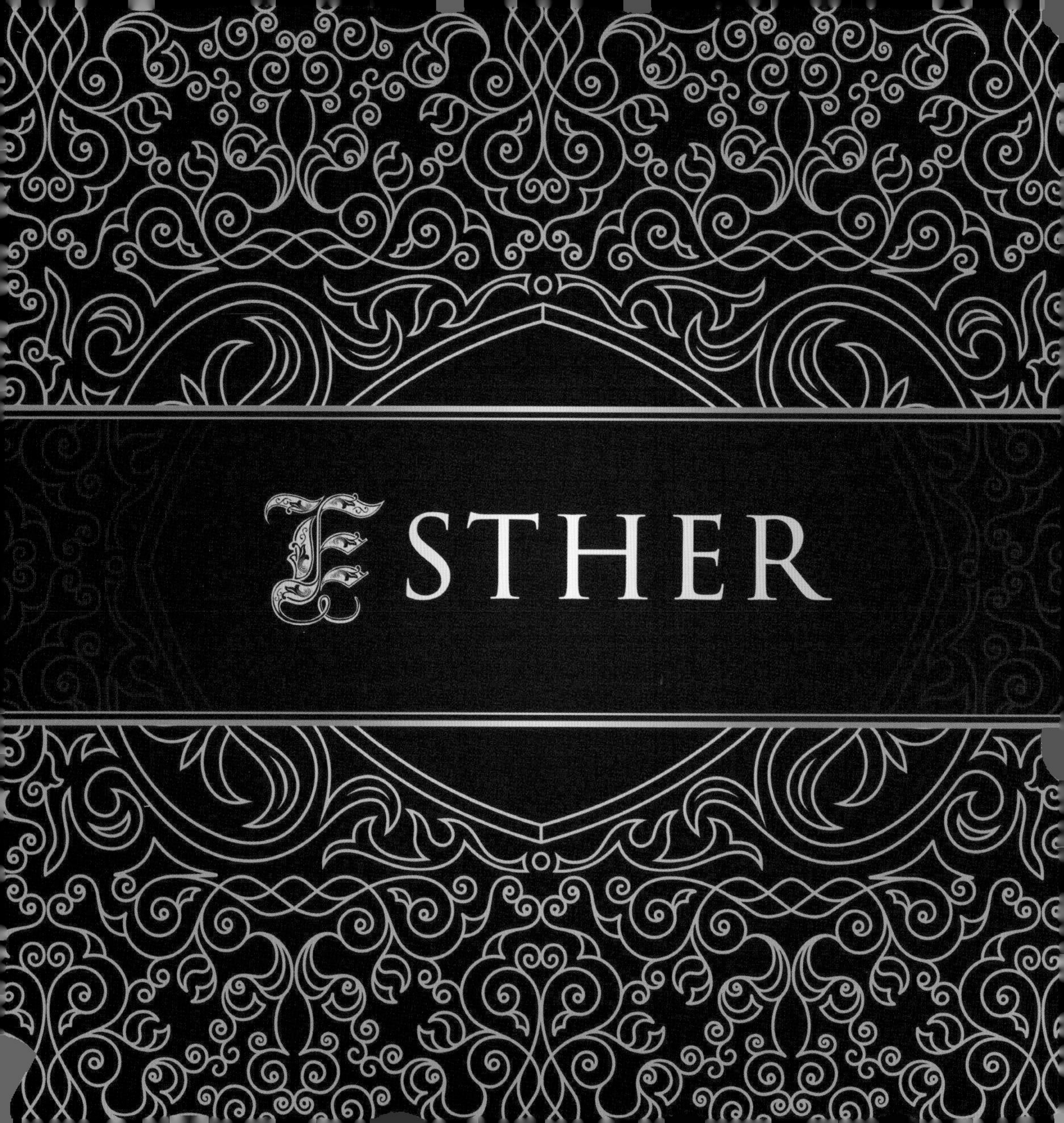
ESTHER

sther is one of the strangest books in the Bible—a book with no overt mention of God. Yet behind the events is the unmistakable hand of God's providence—His ruling and overruling of circumstances. Esther was a Jewish woman who rose to the Persian throne through an unlikely series of events. When she learned her people were endangered throughout the empire, she overcame her fears to enact a plan to save them. With the help of her relative Mordecai, Esther defeated the plot of her enemies and delivered the Jews from a massacre.

Our lives sometimes seem to go off script with unlikely situations, difficult plots, dark moments, and confusing circumstances. Sometimes it's difficult to see God's overt plan as the days unfold one after the other. But the message of Esther—and indeed, of the whole Bible—is that God is involved in all the details of organizing, synchronizing, ruling, and overruling.

Romans 8:28 tells us that all things will work together for good in the lives of those who love the Lord, but we aren't told how or when—simply that they will. We must trust God's providence to weave together all the strands and combine the colors into the picture He's developing.

Theologian B. B. Warfield said, "A firm faith in the universal providence of God is the solution of all earthly troubles." And James Russell Lowell said, "Behind the dim unknown, standeth God with the shadow, keeping watch above his own."

That's the message of Esther for us!

KEY THEME:

Trust the hidden resources of God's providence when you are unable to see visible solutions to life's dilemmas.

KEY CHALLENGE:

Actively do your part to be of help to others during difficulties, but trust in the knowledge that God will be doing His much greater part!

KEY VERSE:

"Yet who knows whether you have come to the kingdom for such a time as this?" (Esther 4:14)

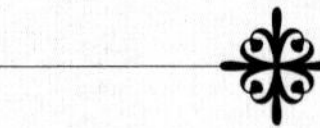

KEY PRAYER:

Father, help me to trust You even when I don't understand what is happening in my life or in the world around me.

JOB

he book of Job contains 42 chapters, and the main theme is suffering. The first two chapters set the stage. Job was a righteous and wealthy man whom Satan targeted for special attack. A series of devastating events hit Job, sending everything in his life crashing down. In chapters 3 through 37, his friends tried to reason through his problems with him by suggesting he had sinned in some terrible way to be so punished. The Lord breaks into the story in chapter 38, telling Job to trust Him who is the Creator of time and eternity, heaven and earth. As Job learned the lessons and prayed for his friends, his conditions changed, and his new prosperity exceeded even what he had before.

Throughout the book, Job chose to trust God. One of the deepest expressions of faith in all of Scripture is Job 13:15, "Though He slay me, yet will I trust Him." In other words, Job said, "Even if the Lord takes everything away from me, ravages me, and kills me, I have no better option and no greater desire than to trust that in the end it will make sense and He will care for me."

Not all our prayers are answered as we'd like, and everyone's life contains adversity. Some events in life can devastate us. But God still reigns with sovereignty from His throne. We have no better option and no greater desire than to trust Him.

KEY THEME:

Trust God even when you are suffering. He is sovereign over our lives and our future.

KEY CHALLENGE:

Trust the Lord enough to say, "Thy will be done!" even when life's circumstances seem overwhelming.

KEY VERSE:

"Though He slay me, yet will I trust Him" (Job 13:15).

KEY PRAYER:

God, thank You that when my world is falling apart, I can trust in Your perfect plan for me.

PSALMS

he ancient Hebrew title for this book is "Praises!" The word *Psalms* comes from a Greek word meaning "to pluck the strings," indicating the 150 units in this book are songs. They are poetical, theological, emotional, covering almost every life condition imaginable. In some of the Psalms, the writer is battling despair; in others he is shouting from the heights of joy.

This book was compiled over time in five great sections: Book 1 (Psalms 1–41), Book 2 (Psalms 42–72), Book 3 (Psalms 73–89), Book 4 (Psalms 90–106), Book 5 (Psalms 107–150). The ancient Hebrews knew most or all these songs by heart and sang them in their worship, in their synagogues, in their homes, and in their travels to Jerusalem for the great festivals.

Many of the Psalms are attributed to David, who established the liturgies and forms for temple worship in Old Testament days.

All believers need songs in their hearts. God created music as a gift to us. Even if we're not musicians, we can internalize the great music of the Bible and of the Church. Sometimes a psalm, hymn, or spiritual song will help us as no spoken word can. Having a collection of lifetime lyrics is critical for spiritual health.

The Psalms are ideal for memorizing, and a mind filled with verses from this vast collection will be tuned to sing God's praises. Worship is an essential element of emotional and spiritual health. So make a joyful noise unto the Lord. Serve Him with gladness and come before His presence with singing (Psalm 100:1-2)

KEY THEME:

Celebrate God's presence in worship,
music, and praise.

KEY CHALLENGE:

Make memorizing joyful verses from the book of Psalms a part of your regular Bible study. Keep them close to your heart and mind so that the joy of the Lord can be your strength throughout each day.

KEY VERSE:

"Make a joyful shout to the Lord, all you lands! Serve the Lord with gladness; come before His presence with singing" (Psalm 100:1-2).

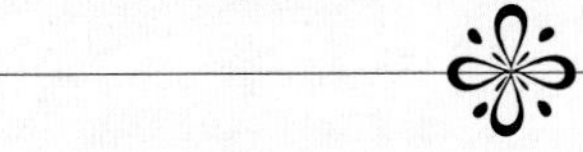

KEY PRAYER:

Lord, I thank You and praise You today for who You are and for all You have done for me!

PROVERBS

ometimes you need truth on the run. The book of Proverbs contains about five hundred bits of portable truth. Each one adds to our wisdom about how to go about our daily lives. With the Proverbs of Solomon, we can grab one and run into the day with it.

God's wisdom isn't reflected as much in academic degrees as in blameless living. The book of Proverbs deals with life's most practical issues—working hard, eating moderately, living honestly, and making good decisions on matters great and small. Proverbs warns us against sexual immorality, boastful talking, and hateful gossip. They exhort us to self-control.

As often observed, there are 31 chapters in Proverbs—a chapter for each day of the month. The topics in Proverbs aren't organized topically but are scattered throughout the book because every passing day brings us face to face with the challenges they address.

Though Proverbs covers scores of subjects and hundreds of life's details, they aren't a disconnected series of miscellaneous axioms. They all flow from one source—the fear of the Lord. There's only one way to live wisely in our behavior, attitudes, words, and habits. It's by acknowledging God in all His attributes. He is holy, powerful, sovereign, wise, loving, just, eternal, and always present. Fearing Him means standing in awe of His glorious splendor, unwilling to live in a way that violates His character.

The fear of the Lord is the beginning of wisdom, and wisdom is the beginning of a healthy and holy life that brings glory to God in every daily detail.

KEY THEME:

Treasure God's Word and commands within you. Incline your ear to His wisdom and your heart to understanding His leading.

KEY CHALLENGE:

Read the chapter in Proverbs that corresponds to the day of the month! You'll read Proverbs through each month of the year!

KEY VERSE:

"The fear of the Lord is the beginning of wisdom, and the knowledge of the Holy One is understanding" (Proverbs 9:10).

KEY PRAYER:

Lord, help me keep my thoughts and actions focused on You, walking in Your wisdom and Your Word rather than the wisdom and ways of the world.

ECCLESIASTES

cclesiastes is a book of philosophy. King Solomon viewed the futility of life without God, and he described where he himself had gone wrong. His purpose was that we might learn from his mistakes and choose a philosophy of life that leads to joy. That philosophy means adopting a biblical worldview—that God exists and must be feared, obeyed, and followed. Without Him, life is void, empty, meaningless, and sad.

This is one of the Bible's more difficult books to analyze and interpret, but the central lesson involves *meaning* in life. We will never find fulfillment in riches, fame, accomplishment, or position, for all those things are temporary. We are made with eternity in our hearts (Ecclesiastes 3:11), and we need the kind of eternal significance that comes only with a personal connection with our Creator.

Solomon is writing especially for young people; he tells them this: "Remember now your Creator in the days of your youth" (12:1). He closes his book with this summation: "Let us hear the conclusion of the whole matter: Fear God and keep His commandments, for this is man's all. For God will bring every work into judgment, including every secret thing, whether good or evil" (12:13-14).

Each of us has a personal philosophy about life, even if we've never taken a university class in philosophy. What mindset really works? What way of thinking produces joy? How do we find personal and eternal significance? Praise God, it is available and found in an abiding relationship with our loving Creator!

KEY THEME:

Fulfillment in life is not found in riches or possessions, but in trusting God not only for today but for eternity. He alone brings meaning to every area of life.

KEY CHALLENGE:

Any accomplishment in this world is temporary, so the only real significance in life is found in God's eternal purposes. Make it a goal to pursue the things in life that will last, for they will yield joy in this life and the next.

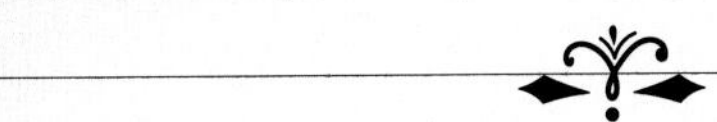

KEY VERSE:

"I know that whatever God does, it shall be forever.... God does it, that men should fear before Him" (Ecclesiastes 3:14).

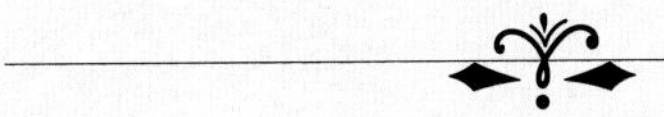

KEY PRAYER:

Father, help me to keep my focus on You, to avoid the distractions of the world that only bring futility and hopelessness, and to remember that the true meaning and purpose in life is found only in You.

SONG OF SOLOMON

ike his father, Solomon was a musician and songwriter, the author of 1,005 songs (1 Kings 4:32). This one is preserved in the Bible, and its theme is love. Especially the love between a husband and wife. Though not overly explicit in a literal way, Song of Solomon uses figures of speech to describe the sanctity of wedded love.

In the story, King Solomon traveled from Jerusalem to the areas north, near Nazareth. He saw a Shulamite woman and fell in love with her. He wrote this poem about their courtship and marriage. The tale is told by various characters—the bride, groom, and their friends. It shows us that God designed marriage to be joyful, even if we ourselves are imperfect. In this song, the couple had a serious misunderstanding (Song of Solomon 5:2–6:3), but they worked through it, resolved to let true love prevail.

The writer uses many pictures from nature, including this one in Song of Solomon 2:15: "Catch us the foxes, the little foxes that spoil the vines, for our vines have tender grapes." Our relationships are threatened by little things, by the little foxes. They romp and frolic in the vineyard, and they can ruin the tender vines and immature grapes. It's not just major issues that damage our relationships. Sometimes it's small aggravations, little grievances, and minor flaws.

The Bible teaches that love overcomes and covers a multitude of sins (1 Peter 4:8). Don't focus on the weaknesses of others, but on their strengths. Beware the little foxes!

KEY THEME:

Never let resentments, arguments, neglect, and other "little foxes" nibble away at the romance and health of the home.

KEY CHALLENGE:

Be a person who looks for the good in people rather than focusing on their faults and frailties. Don't allow negativity to play a role in your relationships with your friends and loved ones.

KEY VERSE:

"Many waters cannot quench love, nor can the floods drown it. If a man would give for love all the wealth of his house, it would be utterly despised" (Song of Solomon 8:7).

KEY PRAYER:

God, give me the ability to love others well and to see them as You do, and not to allow sinful pride to enter my relationships with people that I should love.

ISAIAH

saiah is the prince of the prophets, writing eloquently on the greatest themes revealed from heaven. The first part of his book is addressed to those facing the challenge of a military invasion by Assyria (chapters 1–35). The latter chapters are addressed to those who had been exiled during the Babylonian invasion (chapters 40–66). The Lord gave Isaiah advance messages for them that are filled with encouragement. Throughout the book, we find detailed information about the coming Messiah. There's so much about the Lord Jesus in Isaiah that his book is called the Fifth Gospel.

Isaiah's call to ministry is full of lessons for us. In chapter 6, he saw the Lord high and lifted up, exalted and surrounded by the seraphim, who were shouting, "Holy, holy, holy is the Lord of hosts; the whole earth is full of His glory!" (verse 3)

Seeing the Lord enthroned in glorious splendor compelled Isaiah to confess his sins and offer to go forward as the Lord's worker.

Oh, that we could better see the splendor, glory, and majesty of the King! We're prone to think of Him as a good Father, which He is. But He also dwells in the highest heavens and His throne blazes with undiluted holiness. The more we see Him as He is, the more we see ourselves as we are.

Like Isaiah, our twin cries are: "Woe is me" and "Here am I!" (Isaiah 6:5, 8) Our highest motivation for the Lord's work springs from our highest view of His regal and royal exaltation.

KEY THEME:

As God's people we are to live in anticipation of our promised Messiah, to renew our strength in Him, and to willingly proclaim, "Here am I! Send me" (Isaiah 6:8).

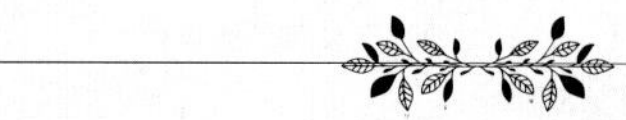

KEY CHALLENGE:

Study the attributes of God, learn more about Him, and resolve to be a dedicated servant of His majesty through your loving service to Him.

KEY VERSE:

"Also I heard the voice of the Lord, saying: 'Whom shall I send, and who will go for Us?' Then I said, 'Here am I! Send me'" (Isaiah 6:8).

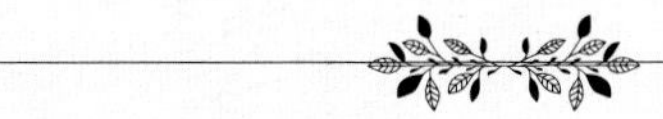

KEY PRAYER:

Lord, give me a heart for others and use me to share the Gospel with those around me. "Here am I! Send me."

JEREMIAH

f you feel you live in discouraging times, you'll sense a partner in the prophet Jeremiah. He lived during the final stages of his nation of Judah. Despite his long and labored efforts, few people responded to his message. Yet he was faithful, and his sermons have sustained the Lord's people for 2,500 years.

The first chapter records God's call for Jeremiah to be a prophet. Chapters 2 through 51 are a collection of his sermons, and chapter 52 records the tragic fall of Jerusalem.

Not everyone lives in times of revival and spiritual prosperity. Sometimes we're called to hard places or hard times. The Lord warned Jeremiah his ministry would often fall on deaf ears. But He said, "Speak to them all that I command you. Do not be dismayed before their faces.... For behold, I have made you this day a fortified city and an iron pillar, and bronze walls against the whole land.... They will fight against you, but they shall not prevail against you. For I am with you" (Jeremiah 1:17-19).

This sounds discouraging, but truly it's comforting. We're not responsible for how the culture reacts to the message of Christ. We're simply responsible to be faithful in doing as the Lord commands. He alone can manage the results. If our message seems to fall on hardened hearts, it's comforting to know Jeremiah faced the same thing. Yet God used him in ways he couldn't imagine. Even today, the Lord speaks to us through this poignant book.

Our labor in the Lord is never in vain!

KEY THEME:

God will be our God and we must be His people, going where He sends us and speaking whatever He tells us, regardless of visible results.

KEY CHALLENGE:

Wave off any discouragement that enters your life. Choose instead to be encouraged in the Lord—He will faithfully bless your efforts for His glory.

KEY VERSE:

"But the Lord said to me: 'Do not say, "I am a youth," for you shall go to all to whom I send you, and whatever I command you, you shall speak'" (Jeremiah 1:7).

KEY PRAYER:

Lord, grant me courage and boldness to share Christ with my family, friends, and neighbors and to remember that any work that I do for You will not be in vain.

LAMENTATIONS

he five chapters of Lamentations are a heavy dark frame around the bright picture drawn in the middle of the book in Lamentations 3:21-24. Jeremiah wrote these chapters as funeral dirges for his Jerusalem, which had fallen to the Babylonians. The first chapter is a poem describing the cry of the defeated city. Chapter 2 explains the role of the judgment of God. The third chapter records Jeremiah's response to what he saw. The last two chapters tell us why judgment fell and what the nation should do next.

It's a weary and dark set of verses, but it's no accident that a picture of grace bursts from the middle of the book: "This I recall to my mind, therefore I have hope. Through the Lord's mercies we are not consumed, because His compassions fail not. They are new every morning; great is Your faithfulness. 'The Lord is my portion,' says my soul, 'therefore I hope in Him!'" (Lamentations 3:21-24)

In times of sorrow and suffering, we must learn to do as Jeremiah did, to bring God's faithfulness to mind. God's compassion and mercy never falter, even in desperate times. If we simply focus on the sadness around us, we'll sink into depression. But if we look around and see the Lord, we'll find a lifeline that will pull us upward in hope and understanding.

If you're lamenting something in your life today, it's understandable. Life is full of sad moments. But even now, bring this to mind and have hope: His compassions never cease; they are new every morning.

Great is His faithfulness.

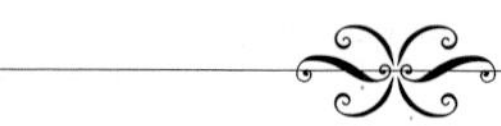

KEY THEME:

Like Jeremiah in his distress, we must lift our thoughts from despair and open the windows of our mind, recalling the wonders of the God in whom we hope.

KEY CHALLENGE:

Even in moments of sadness and despair, there is hope to be found in God. Find something in the midst of your circumstances that proves the faithfulness of God to you at this very moment and praise Him for His faithfulness to you.

KEY VERSE:

"His compassions fail not. They are new every morning; great is Your faithfulness" (Lamentations 3:22-23).

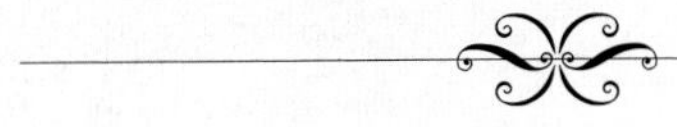

KEY PRAYER:

Heavenly Father, thank You for Your faithfulness to me each day! Thank You for Your unfailing compassion that is new every day. You are a good and faithful Father.

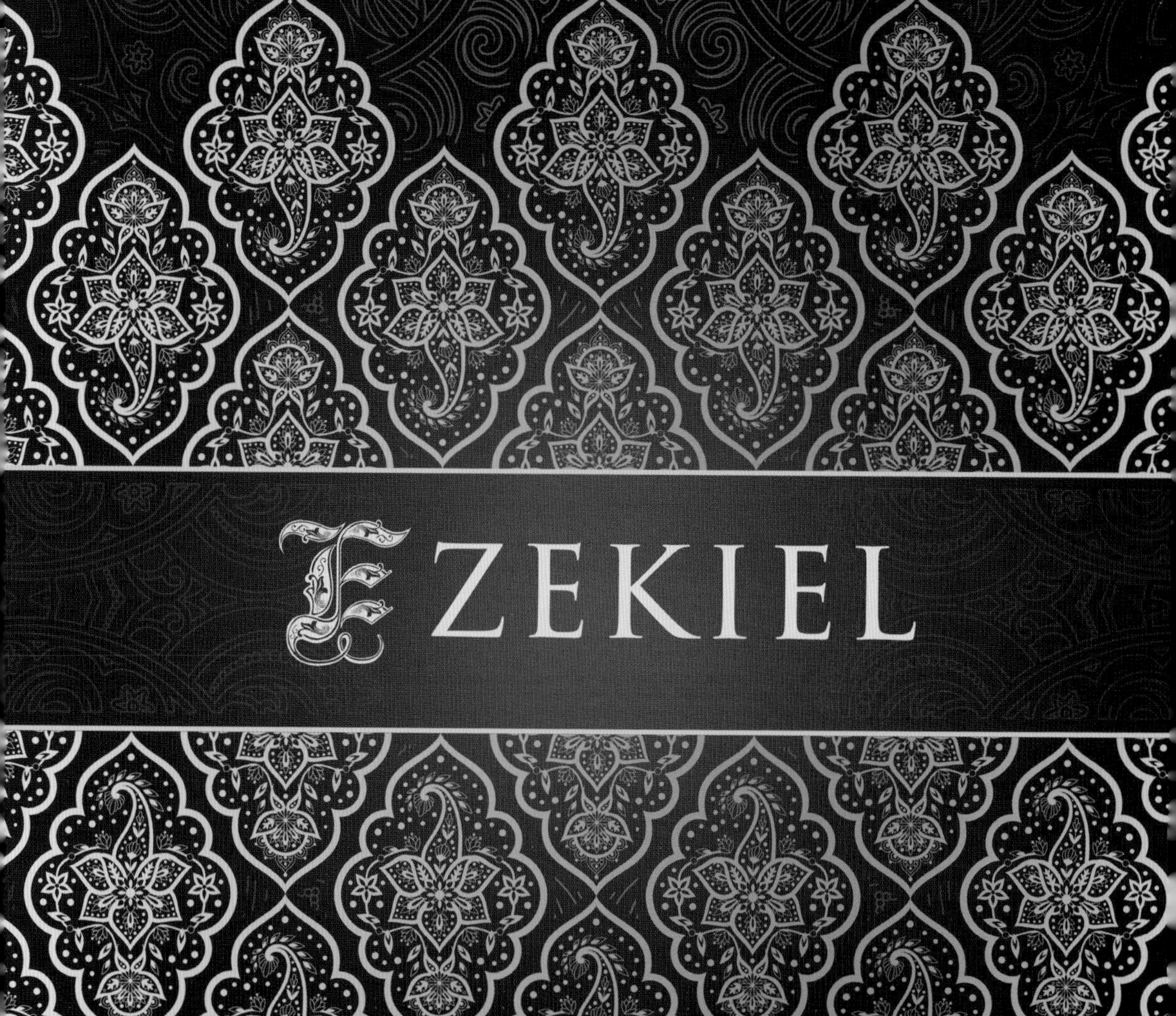

EZEKIEL

zekiel was God's prophet to the exiles in Babylon during the final days of the nation of Judah, and his book is divided into two distinct sections. The first 32 chapters of Ezekiel warn the exiles that Jerusalem will be destroyed, which was a reality they could not accept. They thought the Lord's glory in Jerusalem would preserve the city forever. Ezekiel, however, knew that the Lord's glory was departing due to the sins of the people (see Ezekiel 8–11).

After news came of the destruction of Jerusalem, Ezekiel's message radically changed. Chapters 33 through 48 describe the future of God's people when the glory will return to Jerusalem and the Messiah will reign in peace and victory. During this time of coming glory, the Lord will put a new heart in His people. They will be indwelled by the Spirit and walk in His statutes (Ezekiel 36:26-27).

We can have that experience now! We needn't wait for the millennial reign of Christ. When we receive Him as our Savior, He gives us a new heart, fills us with His Spirit, and enables us to walk in His statutes. The glory of God shines through our lives. The Bible says, "Christ in you, the hope of glory" (Colossians 1:27).

Not everyone wants to hear our message, but they can't deny the radiant-filled hope of those who have a new heart, an obedient life, the indwelling Spirit, and a glorious future. Let's show the world what that looks like!

KEY THEME:

We must speak God's words to our generation, whether they hear or whether they refuse to listen, showing them that we have hope because of His love and indwelling Spirit in our lives.

KEY CHALLENGE:

Think of the wonder of God's indwelling Spirit in your life. Rejoice in that wonderful knowledge! Let the light of His love and glory be evident to others through you.

KEY VERSE:

"I will give you a new heart and put a new spirit within you; I will take the heart of stone out of your flesh.... I will put My Spirit within you and cause you to walk in My statutes" (Ezekiel 36:26-27).

KEY PRAYER:

Dear God, thank You for the knowledge that You are the answer to the world's deepest questions. Help me to boldly share You and Your love with those who are desperately searching for answers today.

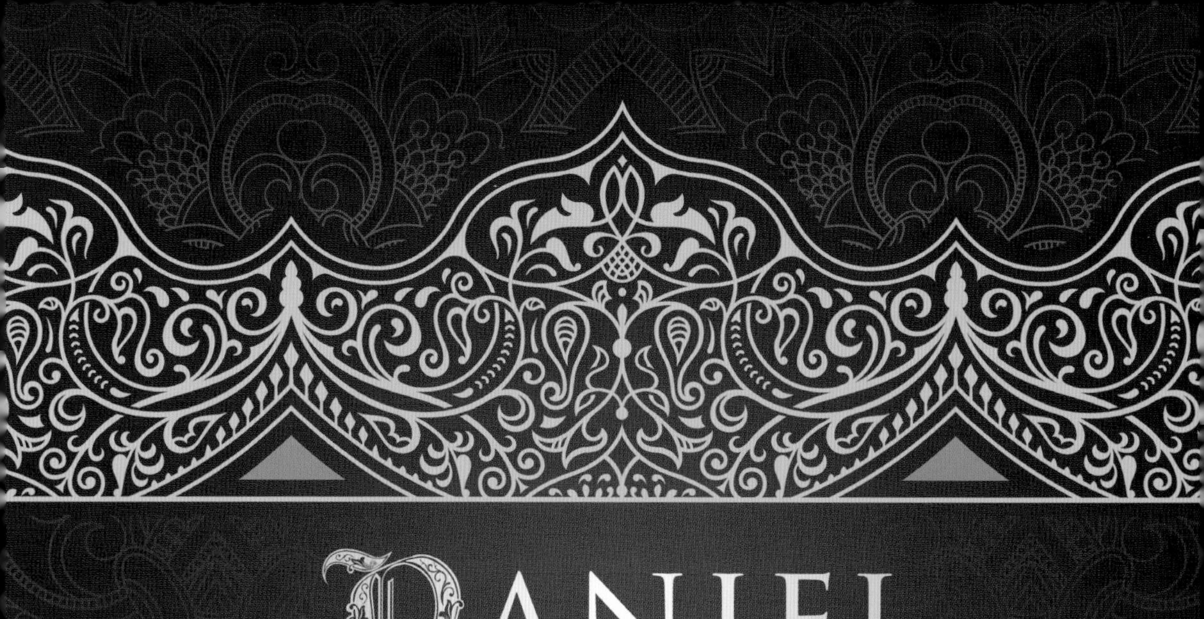

DANIEL

aniel was probably a teenager when he became one of the first inhabitants of Jerusalem to be seized and marched by the Babylonians into exile. His maturity exceeded his years, and he remained steadfast to the Lord at every point, diligently studying the Scriptures (Daniel 9:1-2), remaining close to his God-fearing friends (2:17-18), and praying three times a day (6:10). The Lord rewarded Daniel with political power to influence those around him, and, most of all, with powerful revelations about the future.

We can be just as faithful to the Lord as Daniel, especially if we follow his example of daily Bible study, fellowship, and prayer. Plus, we have all the prophecies the Lord gave him. We should study his prophetic announcements just as diligently as he studied the prophecies of Jeremiah (9:1-2).

Daniel's predictions provide a blueprint for all biblical prophecy, and they infuse our hearts with a hopeful longing for the events leading to the return of Christ. We can become people who live in the prophetic future. We even understand these things better than Daniel did because we have all the New Testament predictions to enlighten the picture.

We also know the "Most High rules in the kingdom of men" (Daniel 4:25).

The things of earth will fade as we set our minds on "One like the Son of Man, coming with the clouds of heaven.... His dominion is an everlasting dominion, which shall not pass away" (Daniel 7:13-14).

KEY THEME:

We must serve God faithfully, remaining undefiled in a godless society, living prophetically in the future.

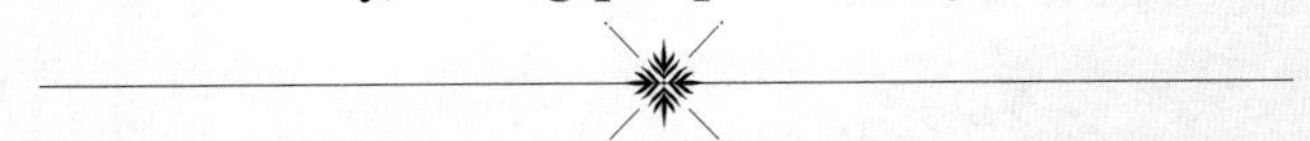

KEY CHALLENGE:

The kingdoms of this world will ultimately fade into obscurity. But while we are here, enjoy the splendor of God's creation in sunrises, sunsets, starlit skies, lightning bolts and more, reflecting upon the Lord's return and praying, "Even so, come, Lord Jesus!" (Revelation 22:20)

KEY VERSE:

"Blessed be the name of God forever and ever, for wisdom and might are His" (Daniel 2:20).

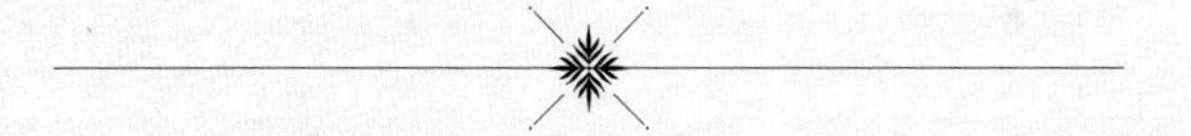

KEY PRAYER:

Lord, help me to faithfully live a life of service to You, regardless of my culture, where I live, or my circumstances, as I eagerly anticipate Your return.

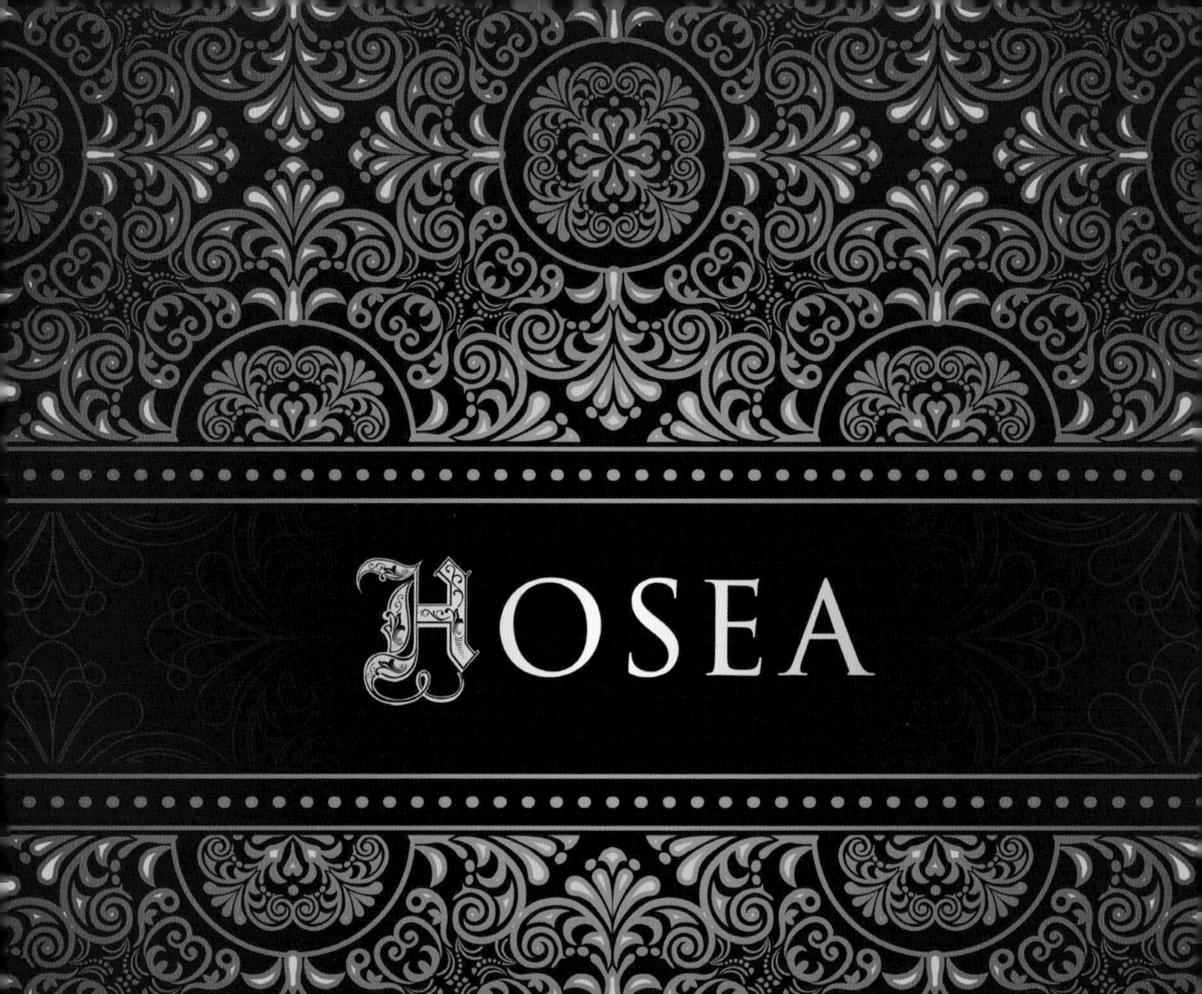

HOSEA

hen we open Hosea's book, we find three chapters describing his own difficult marriage. The remainder of the book—chapters 4 through 14—is a selection of emotional lessons in which God expressed His anguish over Israel's spiritual adultery. The Lord begged Israel to turn back to Him with exclusive devotion like a true wife, and He promised a full and glorious reconciliation and restoration.

The whole book is summed up in Hosea 10:12, where the Lord told Israel to engage in some personal farming. They needed to tend to their spiritual garden by breaking up their fallow ground. The word *fallow* refers to ground that was plowed but left unseeded for a growing cycle. It has since become hardened and needs to be broken up again.

Our hearts can become hardened so quickly! Like a farmer, we must cultivate them like a field, planting seeds of righteousness.

In other words, we must tend to our habits and strive for personal holiness in all that we do. The Lord Himself will send the showers of blessings and reap a harvest of righteousness.

Hosea, then, presents two ways to consider the state of our relationship with the Lord. We should be a faithful loving wife—the Bride of Christ. And we should be a well-tended garden, producing the fruit of the Spirit.

If you were a gardener given a piece of land—your heart—is there any ground that needs to be broken up? Any weeds to be pulled? Any seeds to sow?

Think about it!

KEY THEME:

It's time to seek the Lord and to serve Him faithfully until He returns and showers His righteousness on us.

KEY CHALLENGE:

Sow the seeds of righteousness in your mind by finding a Bible verse to memorize, recall, and live out in your life. Regularly repeat the verse to yourself and record it in a journal or a note.

KEY VERSE:

"Sow for yourselves righteousness; reap in mercy; break up your fallow ground, for it is time to seek the Lord, till He comes and rains righteousness on you" (Hosea 10:12).

KEY PRAYER:

Father, I rejoice in Your blessings to me. Help me to keep the garden of my heart well-tended and the soil of my life easily cultivated with Your Truth. My prayer is that I will come to know You more deeply as I walk with You each day.

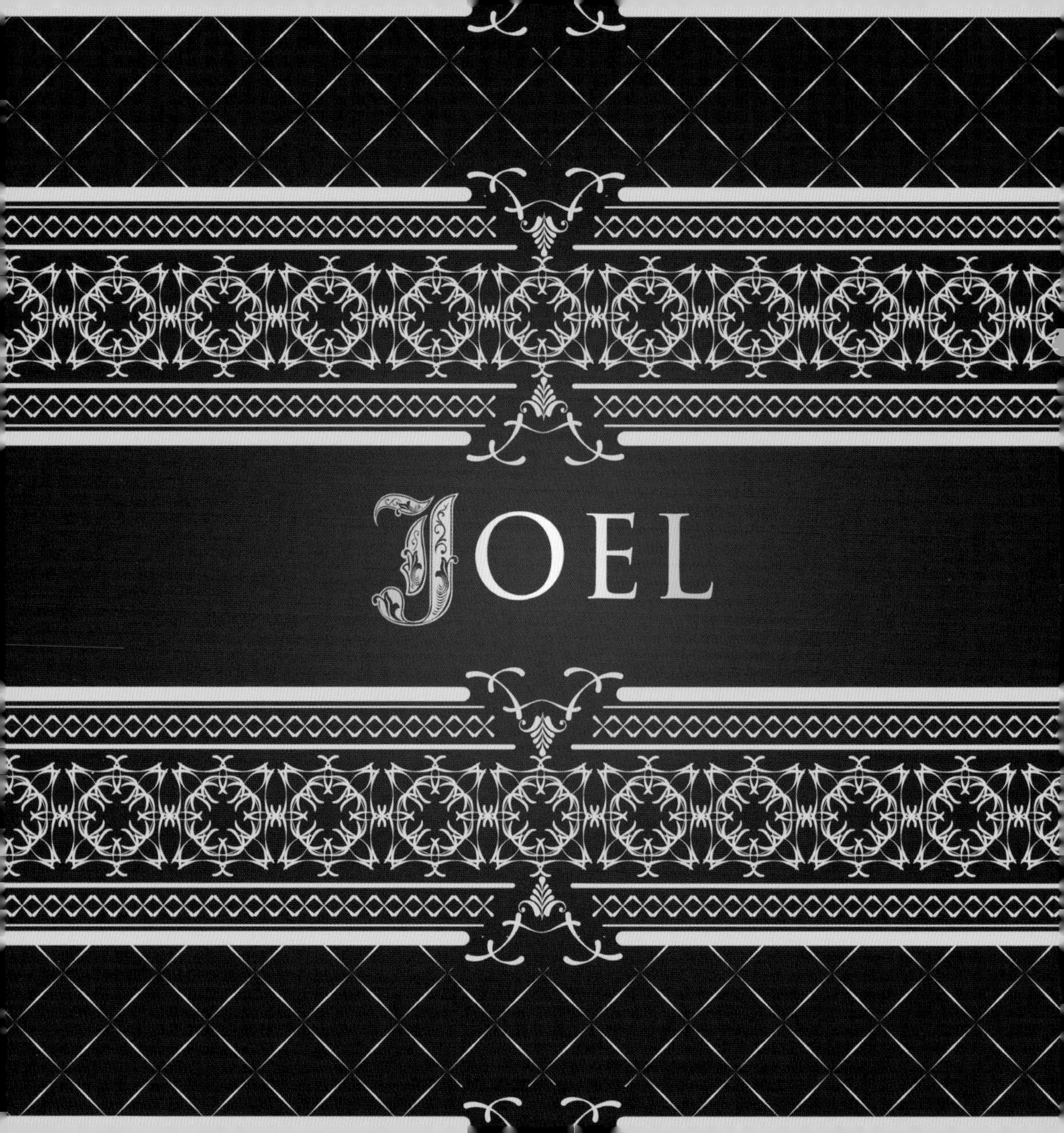
JOEL

eople who study the book of Joel should watch an online video of a locust invasion to visualize the backdrop of his ministry. Thick clouds of the little creatures swarmed across his land, devouring all vegetation in their path. Joel saw it as divine judgment, and he exhorted repentance. He also promised that repentance would bring blessings and that God would "restore to you the years that the swarming locust has eaten" (Joel 2:25).

Starting with Joel 2:28, the prophet jumped to the distant future. The locust invasion of his day was a miniature preview of tribulation events leading to Armageddon and the return of Christ, when the Lord will roar from Zion, shaking the heavens and becoming a shelter and strength for His people (Joel 3:16).

Perhaps Joel's best-known prediction is: "And it shall come to pass afterward that I will pour out My Spirit on all flesh; your sons and your daughters shall prophesy, your old men shall dream dreams, your young men shall see visions" (Joel 2:28).

Partially fulfilled on the Day of Pentecost, this prophecy will be totally accomplished when Jesus returns, turning His Jewish people to their Messiah and pouring the Holy Spirit upon them without measure (see Zechariah 12:10).

Until then, we who know Christ are receptacles for the outpoured Pentecostal Spirit. We are His vessels, and nothing in our lives—not a single locust—should grieve or quench the Spirit within us. Walking in the fullness of the Spirit is an opportunity to be celebrated and experienced!

KEY THEME:

Turn to God and away from any and every sin, for He abundantly pardons and wonderfully restores. He makes all things new.

KEY CHALLENGE:

Don't allow the locusts to devour the work of the Lord in your life. Make it a daily prayer and desire to proclaim: "Lord, fill me to overflowing with Your Spirit!"

KEY VERSE:

"Turn to Me with all your heart, with fasting, with weeping, and with mourning.... And it shall come to pass afterward that I will pour out My Spirit on all flesh" (Joel 2:12, 28).

KEY PRAYER:

Father, thank You for the confidence and knowledge that You restore what is lost when I confess my sin to You. I know that with repentance comes forgiveness and blessing. Thank You for the joy of walking in the fullness of Your Spirit.

AMOS

rue faith is very practical. It results in good deeds, kindness, charity, and justice. None of that was happening in the Northern Kingdom of Israel, so God sent a plain-spoken farmer from the Southern Kingdom to confront them—Amos. He arrived in the North during a golden age of economic prosperity, but beneath the surface there was inequity, injustice, and idolatry. Amos accused the people of vile sins, and he warned them about losing their compassion during their prosperity. "Woe to you who are at ease in Zion.... Who lie on beds of ivory, stretch out on your couches, eat lambs from the flock... who sing idly to the sound of stringed instruments... who drink wine from bowls, and anoint yourselves with the best ointments, but are not grieved for the affliction of Joseph" (Amos 6:1-6).

They were unconcerned about the spiritual ruin of their nation.

What a lesson! Many of us are living in affluent times. We have nice beds and linens, an abundance of food, and cluttered cosmetic trays. We can be thankful for the provisions God sends, but uppermost on our minds should be our need for revival. Millions of people die each year without Christ.

The Lord doesn't call everyone to take a vow of poverty, but each of us should focus on eternal values. Our mission should include caring for the poor, helping those needing justice, and taking the Good News to those who are hungry for the Gospel. May the Lord give us a compassion that reflects His love for the world.

KEY THEME:

Our religious practices are worthless unless we treat others with integrity and compassion.

KEY CHALLENGE:

Determine to put your faith into action. Is there a "luxury" you can sacrifice in order to better support the work of the Gospel? Make sharing Christ a priority in your life.

KEY VERSE:

"Seek good and not evil, that you may live; so the Lord God of hosts will be with you, as you have spoken. Hate evil, love good; establish justice in the gate. It may be that the Lord God of hosts will be gracious to the remnant of Joseph" (Amos 5:14-15).

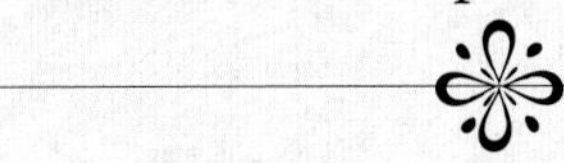

KEY PRAYER:

Lord, give me a heart of compassion for others, to do good with no expectation in return, and allow the people around me to see You through my words and actions.

OBADIAH

t only takes a few minutes to read the book of Obadiah. Little is known about him, but he came alongside Judah to condemn the enemy across the Jordan River—the nation of Edom. The Edomites lived in the high mountains across from Israel, and they inhabited cities carved from stone. The city of Petra is a more recent example.

The Edomites should have been on good terms with Israel, for they were relatives. In the Old Testament, the patriarch Isaac had two sons—Jacob and Esau. The descendants of Jacob became the people of Israel, and the Edomites descended from Esau. But Esau had rejoiced at Israel's misfortunes. One striking verse contains this warning: "But you should not have gazed [gloated over] on the day of your brother in the day of his captivity; nor should you have rejoiced over the children of Judah in the day of their destruction" (Obadiah 1:12).

We can sin with our attitudes. When down, we can grow bitter. When up, we can gloat. When we feel an inward smugness or a root of bitterness, we should confess it as sin. It's one thing to rejoice when justice prevails, but it's another one to withhold compassion for the person or people involved. In all things, we must prayerfully trust God and leave the end result with Him.

As we walk with the Lord in the light of His Word, we grow into godly maturity. Don't be like the Edomites—gloating over their enemy's misfortunes—show compassion to others, even someone who opposes you.

KEY THEME:

When you feel mistreated by others or when others experience failure, work hard to maintain an attitude of compassion toward them.

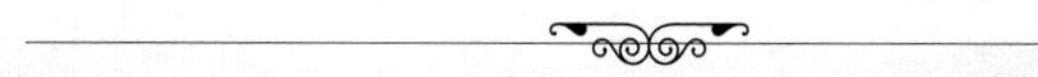

KEY CHALLENGE:

Show compassion to others, even those you don't agree with, especially when they are encountering difficulties or trials in their life.

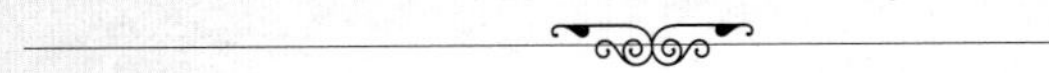

KEY VERSE:

"The pride of your heart has deceived you, you who dwell in the clefts of the rock, whose habitation is high; you who say in your heart, 'Who will bring me down to the ground?'" (Obadiah 1:3)

KEY PRAYER:

Lord, You are a righteous and just Judge, full of compassion. May I show Your compassion and understanding to others and be neither bitter nor gloating toward people who may oppose me and my faith.

JONAH

ave you ever hesitated to turn anything over to the Lord for fear He will work in a way different from what you want?

Jonah did.

Jonah had two problems. The first one, in chapters 1 and 2 of his book, concern his outward rebellion. He flatly said "No" when the Lord told him to go to his archenemies, the Ninevites, and evangelize to them. The Lord responded to that by sending a storm and a big fish.

Jonah's second problem is explored in the last two chapters. Here he outwardly obeyed the Lord, going to Nineveh and preaching. But inwardly, he had no compassion for the people to whom God was sending him. Jonah was displeased when they repented. This time the Lord sent a worm to destroy Jonah's shade. When Jonah was more upset over his lost shade than over the lost city, he began to realize that true obedience is inward as well as outward.

The Lord works on the surface of our lives, but He also works deeply within us. We should strive to remain humble before the Lord, letting His priorities be both explicitly and implicitly ours. He not only knows our hearts; He also wants to shape them into versions of His own. With Jonah, the Lord used a big fish, a storm, a ship full of pagan sailors, a vine, and a worm.

In the same way, watch Him use the simple circumstances around you to shape you into His image—and say, "Hallelujah!"

KEY THEME:

Go wherever the Lord sends you without hesitation or vacillation.

KEY CHALLENGE:

If there is an area of your life you're afraid to hand over to the Lord, take a deep breath and give it to Him without reservation. You can trust His will for your life. His will is best.

KEY VERSE:

"When my soul fainted within me, I remembered the Lord" (Jonah 2:7).

KEY PRAYER:

Father, help me be ready and willing to follow You wherever You lead without procrastination, remembering that there is a purpose and a time for the call on my life.

MICAH

icah is a manageable book to read and study—seven chapters, rich in biblical themes. The first five chapters cover a wide range of issues, including judgment (chapter 1), sin (chapters 2 and 3), and restoration (chapters 4 and 5). The last two chapters are something of a conversation between the Lord and His people regarding their spiritual health.

You'll find one verse from Micah quoted frequently by America's Founding Fathers. From the days of the *Mayflower* to the American Revolution, the founders longed to establish a land where people did justly, loved mercy, and walked humbly with their God (Micah 6:8).

One of today's major social issues involves justice on many levels—economic justice, racial justice, social justice, legal justice. Many of those advocating for justice conceive of theories and practices that exclude the Lord. But those of us who follow

Christ should be the world's best advocates for true justice. The Lord wants people treated fairly, impartially, and rightly.

Perhaps you can think of someone who should be treated differently. Is there anything you can do to correct the wrong endured by such a person? If not, how can you show that person the love of God? This was a major theme of Micah, but the issue pervades all Scripture. We should care for the poor, those who are subjected to discrimination, and those who need an advocate.

After all, we have a great Advocate who speaks on our behalf—the Lord Jesus (1 John 2:1).

KEY THEME:

We need to live justly, love mercy, and walk humbly with God.

KEY CHALLENGE:

As a child of God, be attuned to those needing a sympathetic ear and a compassionate heart. Advocate for others and their needs just as God advocates for you.

KEY VERSE:

"He has shown you, O man, what is good; and what does the Lord require of you but to do justly, to love mercy, and to walk humbly with your God?" (Micah 6:8)

KEY PRAYER:

Heavenly Father, help me to live a just, merciful, and humble life that reflects Your love.

NAHUM

torms break upon the lives of God's children, but the Lord is in the storm, controlling it. Nahum 1:3 says, "The Lord has His way in the whirlwind and in the storm, and the clouds are the dust of His feet."

Little is known about the prophet Nahum or his hometown of Elkosh, but his three chapters are full of reassurance and encouragement for the people of God who have been through a storm. The message is aimed at Judah, who had barely survived the onslaught of the Assyrian invasion. The Assyrians were obscenely cruel, and they delighted in committing atrocities against their victims. In Nahum, the Lord predicted the destruction of Assyria and its capital of Nineveh. At the time, Nineveh was the greatest and most fortified city in the world. Yet within a generation, all of Nahum's predictions came true to the letter.

The Bible tells us, "Beloved, do not avenge yourselves, but rather give place to [God's] wrath; for it is written, 'Vengeance is Mine, I will repay,' says the Lord" (Romans 12:19). Sometimes there is no way for us to rectify a wrong that's been committed against us. We've been abused in some way, but we can't get even. We've been hurt, but we can't correct the wrong.

That's when we can kneel in prayer, give the matter to God, and leave room for His wrath—His judicial righteousness, from which no one can escape except through the blood of Christ. The Lord shelters us, and He will do right by us in the end.

KEY THEME:

Though skies are often dark, we must realize
God is not absent from the storm, and He
never loses sight of His children.

KEY CHALLENGE:

When you're angry or troubled about a wrong done to you, give the matter to the Lord, knowing that as our Righteous Judge, He will bring about justice in His time.

KEY VERSE:

"The Lord is good, a stronghold in the day of trouble; and He knows those who trust in Him" (Nahum 1:7).

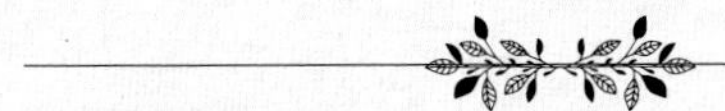

KEY PRAYER:

Dear God, thank You for Your compassionate care in every situation and for being my shelter during the storms of life. When skies are dark, I know I am safe in Your care.

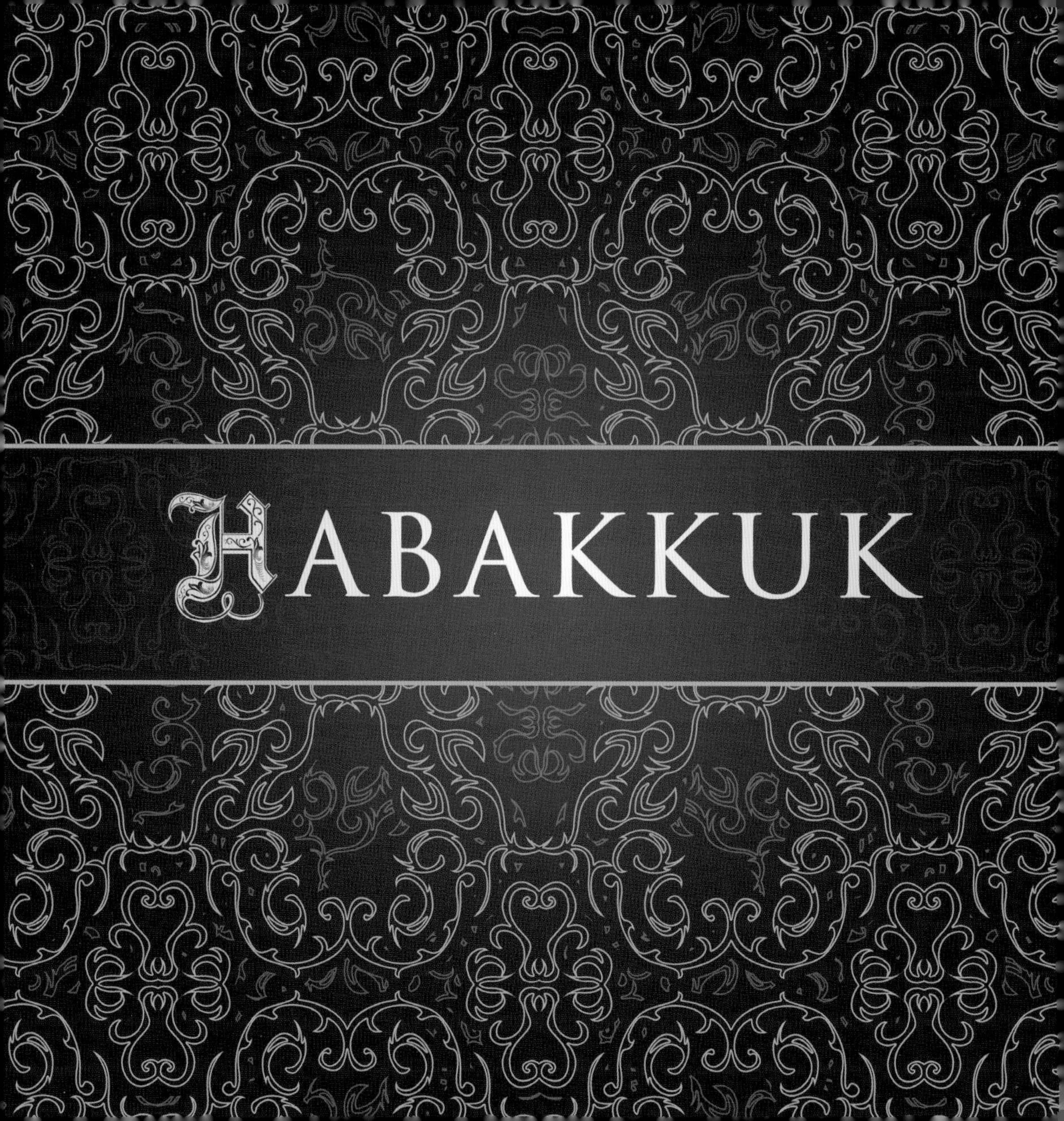
HABAKKUK

he small book of Habakkuk is for people who feel overwhelmed by trouble. It's short and well-organized. In the first two chapters, Habakkuk told the Lord his frustrations. He couldn't understand why God would allow circumstances to collapse around him. The Lord answered, and the two engaged in a conversation. It's helpful to have a version of the Bible that tells you in marginal headings when Habakkuk is speaking and when the Lord is speaking.

In Habakkuk 2:4, the Lord told Habakkuk that godly people must live by faith, a verse that is later quoted in Galatians, Romans, and Hebrews.

As Habakkuk pondered the Lord's responses in chapters 1 and 2, he was encouraged in his ability to trust God. He composed a hymn of faith in chapter 3, and his conclusion is one of the most picturesque expressions of faith in Scripture: "Though the fig tree may not blossom, nor fruit be on the vines; though the labor of the olive may fail, and the fields yield no food...yet I will rejoice in the Lord, I will joy in the God of my salvation" (3:17-18).

How often we're overwhelmed! Our lives are buffeted by troubles, sometimes when we least expect it. We can't walk by sight, but we can walk by faith. We may not be able to rejoice in our lot, but we can rejoice in our Lord, who is our strength and who enables us to walk on a higher plain than we had otherwise known.

KEY THEME:

We are to live by faith, not by sight, fully trusting God even when everything seems to be failing around us.

KEY CHALLENGE:

When you feel troubled and overwhelmed, stop and ask God to give you strength in His Name!

KEY VERSE:

"The Lord God is my strength; He will make my feet like deer's feet, and He will make me walk on my high hills" (Habakkuk 3:19).

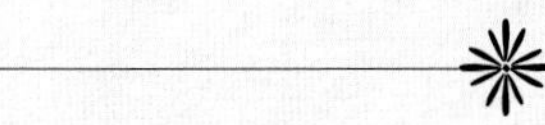

KEY PRAYER:

Lord, even when my life seems to be falling apart around me, thank You for being my shelter and guide. I give You all the glory and praise for I know You are walking with me through every hardship and trial.

ZEPHANIAH

he world won't go on forever, for God has already appointed its last day. That's the message of Zephaniah. The bulk of the book is a warning for people to repent of their sins and seek God with all their heart: "The great day of the Lord is near; it is near and hastens quickly.... A day of wrath, a day of trouble and distress, a day of devastation and desolation" (Zephaniah 1:14-15). Zephaniah warned the people to "seek righteousness, seek humility. It may be that you will be hidden in the day of the Lord's anger" (2:3).

The last chapter ends with an exhortation for those who know the Lord. Let's rejoice in the coming Day, for God's purposes will prevail for His children: "Sing, O daughter of Zion!" (3:14) We're told the Lord is in the midst of His people, singing over them and quieting their troubled hearts with His own nearness.

In an immediate sense, Zephaniah was referring to the Babylonian invasion, but his teachings have their ultimate fulfillment in the days related to the return of Jesus Christ.

The end of the world has never been closer. We're living in the Last Days. The unsaved should look at the future with concern and seek the Savior. Those of us who know Him anticipate our upcoming prospects. We can rejoice in the love of a God who sings over us and who is ready to welcome us into His eternal Kingdom.

You have an inheritance awaiting you!

KEY THEME:

Rejoice in the love of a God who rejoices over you in song.

KEY CHALLENGE:

Live fully in the love of God who brings peace to your troubled mind with His comforting presence.

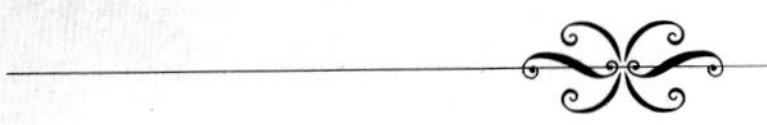

KEY VERSE:

"The Lord your God in your midst, the Mighty One, will save; He will rejoice over you with gladness, He will quiet you with His love, He will rejoice over you with singing" (Zephaniah 3:17).

KEY PRAYER:

Lord, I praise You for Your unfailing and unending love for me. You bring comfort and joy to my heart!

HAGGAI

omeone called discouragement the occupational hazard of ministry. The devil loves to tempt God's servants with discouragement. According to the first chapters of Ezra, that's what happened when the exiles returned to Jerusalem to reestablish the city and rebuild the temple. The work was ill-funded and hard; the progress seemed slow; and the opposition was massive. The people simply gave up and the temple remained in ruins. That is, until the prophets Haggai and Zechariah showed up. Haggai's messages rallied the people, and soon the temple work resumed and was finished in short order.

The book of Haggai gives us the prophet's four short sermons, probably summaries of his longer spoken messages. In the first (Haggai 1:1-15), Haggai rebuked them for building their own houses while the Lord's house remained in ruins. In the second (2:1-9), he exhorted them to be strong and work. Haggai's third message (2:10-19) was a promise from God to bless His people;

and the last one (2:20-23) was a special word of encouragement for the governor of the Jews in Jerusalem, a man named Zerubbabel.

Discouragement slows us down. It robs us of our motivation, our drive, our enthusiasm, and our hopefulness. The encouragement of the Lord is like a blood infusion. When we go about our work with enthusiasm, it's amazing how the Lord will bless!

Put your name in Haggai 2:4: "Yet now be strong, ____________ [your name], says the Lord; ... 'and work; for I am with you.'"

KEY THEME:

Be strong, all you people of the land, and work, for God is with you.

KEY CHALLENGE:

When doing anything for the Lord, put God's priorities before your own comfort. Allow His peace to replace discouragement as you put first things first in your walk with Him.

KEY VERSE:

"'Yet now be strong, Zerubbabel,' says the Lord; 'and be strong, Joshua, son of Jehozadak, the high priest; and be strong, all you people of the land,' says the Lord, 'and work; for I am with you,' says the Lord of hosts" (Haggai 2:4).

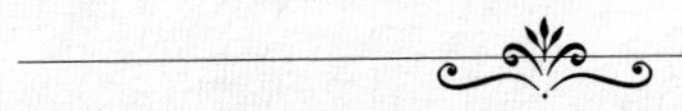

KEY PRAYER:

Lord, strengthen me as I go about the work You have given me to do today. I pray it brings glory and honor to Your Name.

ZECHARIAH

eading Zechariah is good practice for reading the book of Revelation. Both books are full of strange images and apocalyptic language, pointing to the Last Days. Zechariah and Haggai preached side by side as they encouraged the Jewish exiles to finish their work rebuilding the temple. But their messages were different. Haggai spoke in practical terms; Zechariah spoke in visionary language. He anticipated the day when the coming Messiah would inhabit His temple in Jerusalem and reign over all the earth. His details in chapters 11–14 about the coming of Christ give us prophetic information found nowhere else in Scripture.

Perhaps the most helpful of Zechariah's teaching involves the small nature of the Second Temple. Solomon's temple had been the greatest building on earth, a massive edifice for the glory of God. The Babylonians had destroyed it. When the remnant returned and began rebuilding it, it seemed so small and insignificant that many of them wept (Ezra 3:12).

Zechariah told them not do underestimate "the day of small things" (Zechariah 4:10).

Unknown to them, their temple would be expanded by Herod the Great and would become a place of ministry for the Messiah. It was here Jesus was dedicated as a child; here He came at age twelve; here He came as a wise Rabbi to teach the masses.

They were doing their work for Christ!

Little is great when God is in it, and we must never think of our work as insignificant, however it appears to men. Despise not the day of small things.

KEY THEME:

Never be discouraged when the work seems small or slow, for God's Spirit uses little events and unknown people in powerful ways.

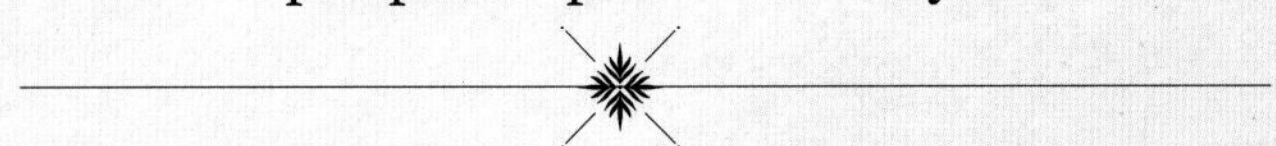

KEY CHALLENGE:

Do something "small" for Christ today
and ask Him to bless it!

KEY VERSE:

"For who has despised the day of small things? For these seven rejoice to see the plumb line in the hand of Zerubbabel. They are the eyes of the Lord, which scan to and fro throughout the whole earth" (Zechariah 4:10).

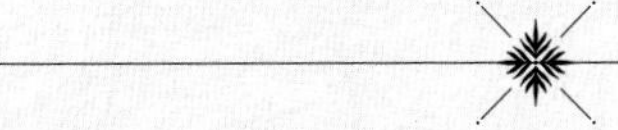

KEY PRAYER:

Heavenly Father, thank You for how You
use the smallest events and the weakest people
to bring glory to Your Name.

MALACHI

pathy! The word comes from the prefix "a," which in Greek creates a negative of the word for *pathos* or *passion*. When we're apathetic, we lose our passion. That's what happened to the people of Israel at the end of the Old Testament. Malachi, the final prophet, came to address that issue. As you read through his little book, you'll see that he used a question-and-answer format to address seven critical issues. When we're apathetic, we doubt God's love, dishonor His name, disrespect His Word, diminish His family, dispute His justice, deprive His work of its needed funds, and demoralize His workers.

What a timely word!

Have you lost your zeal for the Lord? Has an invisible cloud of apathy drifted over your life? Malachi tells us to return to the Lord with fervor and correct every deficiency in our lives.

That includes how we support the Lord's work with our finances. The best-known passage in Malachi says, "'Will a man rob God? Yet you have robbed Me!... In tithes and offerings.... Bring all the tithes into the storehouse, that there may be food in My house, and try Me now in this...If I will not open for you the windows of heaven and pour out for you such blessing that there will not be room enough to receive it'" (Malachi 3:8-10).

We should give with passion, enthusiasm, and gratitude. How wonderful that God allows us to use our tithes and offerings to further His Kingdom in the world! Whatever you do, do it with all your heart!

KEY THEME:

It is time to return with fervor to the Lord, to genuine worship, to high moral values, to marital commitment, and to the practices of tithing and godly fellowship.

KEY CHALLENGE:

Reject apathy and the discouragement that follows it. Make a special gift for the furtherance of the Gospel and discover how little is much when God is in it.

KEY VERSE:

"For I am the Lord, I do not change; therefore you are not consumed, O sons of Jacob. Yet from the days of your fathers you have gone away from My ordinances and have not kept them. Return to Me, and I will return to you" (Malachi 3:6-7).

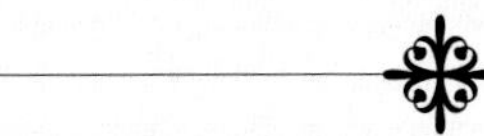

KEY PRAYER:

Lord, I pray that I will live a life worthy of the many blessings You bestow on me each day. You are a good, good Father.

BOOKS OF THE NEW TESTAMENT

MATTHEW

ow did you hear about it? About *Him*? The Gospel only spreads in one way—from person to person. Perhaps you heard through another person's testimony, an article, a book, or sermon. Perhaps you learned at home from your parents or in church from your pastor. Maybe it was a preacher on television or radio, or through a podcast. The important thing is—you heard! And someone needs to hear it from you!

That's the theme of Matthew. The opening book of the New Testament starts with the birth of Christ and the journey of the Wise Men to Jerusalem seeking Him who had been born as a King. As we keep reading, the Gospel unfolds in the biography and teachings of Jesus Christ. For most of the book (chapters 4 through 18), His Galilee ministry is emphasized. From chapters 19 to 28, we see how the story ended in Jerusalem with His final teachings, His death, and His resurrection.

Matthew ends the story there. He doesn't go on to describe the Lord's ascension back into heaven. He purposefully concludes his book with the Risen Christ challenging us to go to all the world and make disciples in all the nations—winning and baptizing them, and then teaching them how to live for Him (Matthew 28:16-20).

Let's make sure the transmission of the Good News doesn't stop with us. As you have heard, so you must tell!

KEY THEME:

Make disciples of all the nations, baptizing them in the name of the Father, of the Son, and of the Holy Spirit.

KEY CHALLENGE:

Discover new and creative ways to embody the Great Commission in your neighborhood, community, and around the world. Take up the cross of Christ and tell someone about the saving grace of Jesus.

KEY VERSE:

"Go therefore and make disciples of all the nations, baptizing them in the name of the Father and of the Son and of the Holy Spirit, teaching them to observe all things that I have commanded you; and lo, I am with you always, even to the end of the age" (Matthew 28:19-20).

KEY PRAYER:

Father, grant me a heart and the opportunity to participate in sharing the Gospel with people around the world.

MARK

f you live in a hurry-up world, you'll appreciate Mark. His book is fast paced, and one of his favorite words is "immediately." That term occurs 36 times in Mark's sixteen chapters: "They immediately left their nets.... And immediately His fame spread throughout all the region.... Immediately many gathered together.... Immediately the girl arose" (Mark 1:18, 28; 2:2; 5:42).

Mark writes with urgency. The first half of his book (1:1–8:30) emphasizes the urgency of knowing who Christ is—the Messiah. The last half (8:31–16:20) is devoted to why He came—to die and rise again—to redeem the world. According to very old traditions, John Mark wrote his Gospel from the recollections of Simon Peter, and Peter was impulsive and impetuous in all he said and did, which helps explain why Mark's words are tinged with urgency.

The urgent tone of Mark's Gospel reflects the compelling mission of the Gospel. We must reach people while we still can—before it's too late. Sociologists tell us 120 people die on earth every minute, which is 172,800 each day.

Think of that! Somewhere on earth, 120 plus people have passed into eternity while you've been reading this page! Furthermore, the mortality rate for every generation is one hundred percent. Every child of God is engaged in a global effort to get the message of Jesus Christ to as many people as quickly as possible. The eternal destiny of millions depends on our sense of urgency.

In a hurry-up world, let's hurry up in getting the Gospel to everyone!

KEY THEME:

When we become disciples of Jesus Christ, we're seized with urgency to serve others and share His Good News with a needy world.

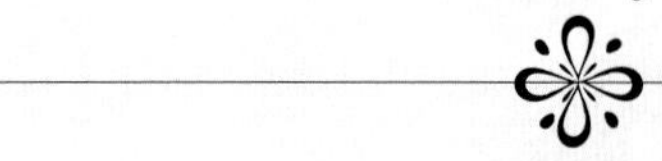

KEY CHALLENGE:

Eternity awaits us all. The question is where we will spend it. Ask God to stir your soul with the urgency of the Gospel and to share your faith with someone you know.

KEY VERSE:

"And He said to them, 'Go into all the world and preach the gospel to every creature'" (Mark 16:15).

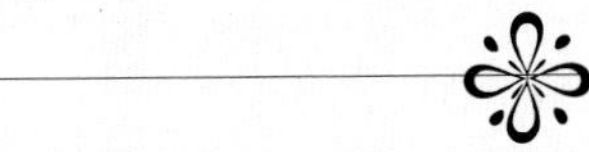

KEY PRAYER:

Lord, I want to be someone who makes a difference in this world. Help me to meet the needs of those around me and to share the Good News with the lost at every opportunity.

LUKE

edical professionals look at life with mercy. Their lives are tied to the hurts, pains, and sorrows of others. That's why Luke is such a vivid writer. He was a physician (Colossians 4:14), and he tenderly described those touched by the ministry of Jesus.

Luke was also a historian, giving us a "narrative of those things which have been fulfilled among us, just as those who from the beginning were eyewitnesses and ministers of the word delivered them to us" (Luke 1:1-2). When you read the third Gospel, you are reading a well-researched biography of Christ.

Luke, then, combines a merciful heart with a head of truth and knowledge. That reflects how we should approach others with the Gospel—with accuracy and with compassion.

People can't believe in their hearts what their minds reject. If they think the Bible is undependable, they can't in good conscience commit their lives to it. But the Bible is dependable, and modern apologetics (the study of the defense of Christianity) has never been as strong or as accessible as it is today. An unbeliever may stump us with a question once, but never twice. Whenever you're confronted with a challenge to the integrity of Scripture, seek out the answer so you'll be ready the next time.

Having a merciful heart is the work of the Holy Spirit as we view the world around us, which is mired in a million needs. Let's have heads full of facts and hearts full of mercy as we seek to win the lost.

KEY THEME:

As followers of Christ, we must be gripped by the needs of lost people, seeking them with the message of life; and rejoicing with the angels when they come to a saving knowledge of our Lord.

KEY CHALLENGE:

Be a faithful student of the Word in preparation to share the Gospel and the hope that is found in Christ to an unbeliever. Be ready!

KEY VERSE:

"Likewise, I say to you, there is joy in the presence of the angels of God over one sinner who repents" (Luke 15:10).

KEY PRAYER:

Lord, this world is in desperate need of You and Your gift of salvation; give me wisdom and the words to speak as I tell others the Good News.

JOHN

ou know how life seems—sometimes slow, sometimes fast. We get a similar sense of the life of Jesus in John's Gospel. The first eleven chapters unfold over a period of three years, with John telling us one story after another of lives touched by the Master. Then the narrative speeds up, with the last half of the book unfolding in the final seven days of our Lord's life, showing us all that took place during Passion Week.

While the entire book of John is holy ground, there's something uniquely sacred about chapter 17, our Lord's private prayer to the Father for Himself, His disciples, and His mission. He began by lifting His eyes to heaven (as He typically did when He prayed), saying, "Father, the hour has come. Glorify Your Son, that your Son also may glorify You.... I have glorified You on the earth. I have finished the work which You have given Me to do" (John 17:1, 4).

In the same way, the hours of our lives are passing in their proper sequence, and we must be about our Father's business seeking to finish the work He has given us to do. Our daily agendas should reflect an awareness that we are God's servants in the Last Days, doing those good works, "which God prepared beforehand that we should walk in them" (Ephesians 2:10).

Let's be like Jesus, who said in John 4:34: "My food is to do the will of Him who sent Me, and to finish His work."

KEY THEME:

Jesus is the way of salvation, offering the invitation to be born again (John 3:7).

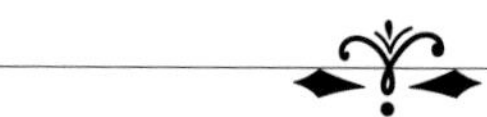

KEY CHALLENGE:

Let the work of God infuse your life's work. Whatever your work is in this life, do it as though you are working for Him, for you are His workmanship, a testimony of His goodness.

KEY VERSE:

"I must work the works of Him who sent Me while it is day; the night is coming when no one can work" (John 9:4).

KEY PRAYER:

Heavenly Father, I praise You for the new life I have in You and for the joy of accomplishing the work You have given me to do.

ACTS

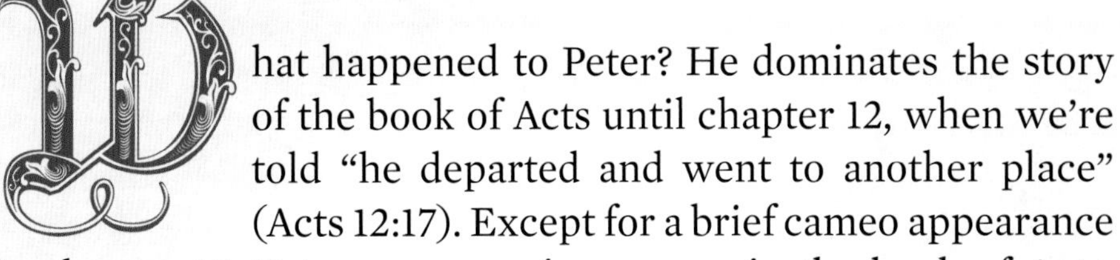

What happened to Peter? He dominates the story of the book of Acts until chapter 12, when we're told "he departed and went to another place" (Acts 12:17). Except for a brief cameo appearance in chapter 15, Peter never again appears in the book of Acts. Instead all the action shifts to the apostle Paul, whose story dominates chapters 13 through 28.

This division in the text actually represents the simplest outline of the book of Acts. Chapters 1–12 revolve around Peter and those working with him, and chapters 13–28 revolve around Paul and those working with him.

There's a lesson here. No single person is a superstar in the work of the Lord, and none of us can do it alone. It's a team effort. The book of Acts shows how the Holy Spirit came upon the followers of Christ, transforming them into one Church, one body, one family, with each member having its own function and role.

You're different from any other Christian on earth. The Lord has given you a unique set of gifts, experiences, opportunities, passions, and personality traits. He takes the diversity of His millions of people and creates a unity that presents the Gospel to the world. It simply won't do if we're not engaged with the Body of Christ, both in our local churches and in His larger Kingdom on earth.

An African-American spiritual says, "If you cannot preach like Peter, if you cannot pray like Paul, you can tell the love of Jesus, who died to save us all."

You have a calling in this life—share Jesus with others!

KEY THEME:

We are called to take the message of the Gospel to the lost wherever they are—it is for everyone!

KEY CHALLENGE:

Be committed to your local church and be part of what His Church is doing around the world. Be a part of the global outreach of the Gospel.

KEY VERSE:

"For we cannot but speak the things which we have seen and heard" (Acts 4:20).

KEY PRAYER:

God, grant me wisdom to know when and where to share the testimony of my faith with others. Please help me to be a winsome witness of Your love and grace to the unsaved.

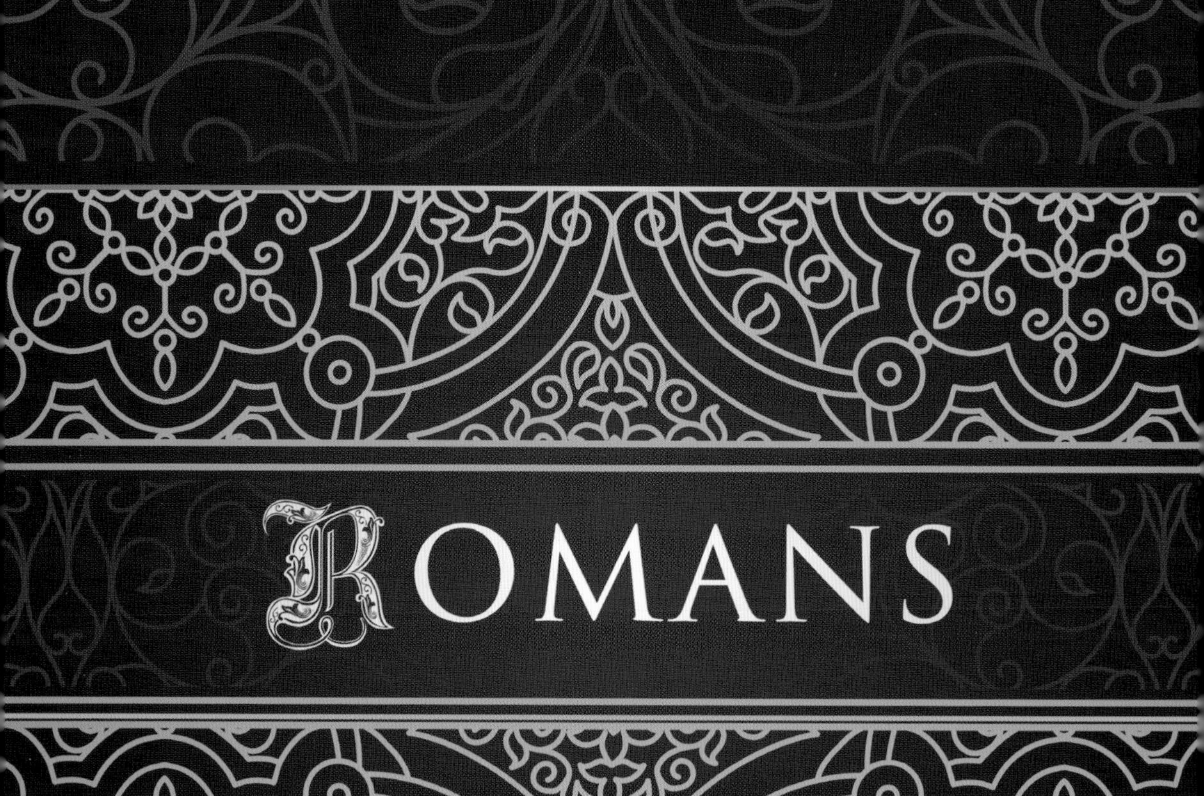
ROMANS

n the 1950s and 60s, thousands of American women wanted to be *Queen for a Day*. That was a popular television show that interviewed various women about their lives and needs, after which the audience voted on who would become *Queen for a Day*. The problem was that most people never won, and the honor only lasted a day.

The book of Romans is God's message to us about reigning in life through Jesus Christ and doing so every day and forever. Because of sin, death reigns in the human experience (Romans 5:14); but because of Christ, grace reigns "through righteousness to eternal life through Jesus Christ our Lord" (verse 21). Through Him, those who receive the "abundance of grace and of the gift of righteousness will reign in life" (verse 17).

Romans is at the heart of biblical theology, explaining the implications of the life, death, and resurrection of Jesus Christ.

Without Romans, we would know the history of our Lord Jesus, but we wouldn't know all the significance that came from His actions. The theme of Romans is justification—that Christ has taken our sins upon Himself and transferred His righteousness to our accounts. We are born into God's Kingdom, adopted into His family, and crowned with eternal life.

It's easy to feel sorry for ourselves and wish that someone would treat us like a king or queen, even if just for a day. But we need to adopt the attitude of Romans 5:17, embracing the glorious truth that we are His royal children, reigning in life.

KEY THEME:

The abundance of God's grace is available to us as believers, which saves us and enables us to reign in life through Christ Jesus.

KEY CHALLENGE:

Reject the reign of sin and death and accept the free gift of God through Jesus Christ and His sacrifice on the cross. No longer a slave to sin you can now claim: "Through Jesus Christ, I can reign in life!" There is victory in Jesus.

KEY VERSE:

"For if by the one man's offense death reigned through the one, much more those who receive abundance of grace and of the gift of righteousness will reign in life through the One, Jesus Christ" (Romans 5:17).

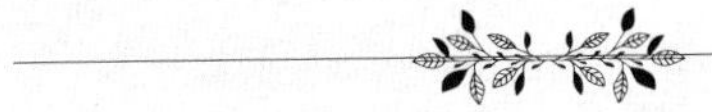

KEY PRAYER:

Father, thank You for the amazing gift of grace that saved me from my sin and made me a member of God's family, His royal child, and more than a conqueror.

I CORINTHIANS

ew things are as painful as church disagreements. It's possible some disagreements are almost unavoidable (even Paul and Barnabas clashed in Acts 15). But every church conflict does damage to us and to our congregation's testimony.

The apostle Paul grieved over the problems in the church of Corinth. He wrote several letters and made repeated visits there. The book of 1 Corinthians sought to address the central issues. The first six chapters discussed quarrels in the church. Starting in chapter 7, Paul answered questions about other issues.

This book should serve as a warning and a preventative to us. We can learn to be healthier by studying the life of someone with unhealthy habits. In the same way, a firm grasp on 1 Corinthians will help us avoid some of their problems.

The best known section of this book is the "Love Chapter" of the Bible—1 Corinthians 13. With understated eloquence, this chapter describes the necessity for love, the characteristics of love, and the eternal nature of the divine *agape*-love God wants to produce in our hearts: "Love suffers long and is kind; love does not envy; love does not parade itself, is not puffed up; does not behave rudely...rejoices in the truth; bears all things, believes all things, hopes all things, endures all things" (1 Corinthians 13:4-7).

When we grow into this kind of love, our conflicts lessen and we can enjoy the unity of the Holy Spirit. A healthy church, like a healthy believer, is growing in the love of Jesus.

KEY THEME:

God is love. The Lord of the Church wants to restore the selfless love and unity that only He can bring to His Church.

KEY CHALLENGE:

Choose today to be a person who is known by love—who suffers long and does not envy—as a sign of your commitment to Christ.

KEY VERSE:

"Though I speak with the tongues of men and of angels, but have not love, I have become sounding brass or a clanging cymbal" (1 Corinthians 13:1).

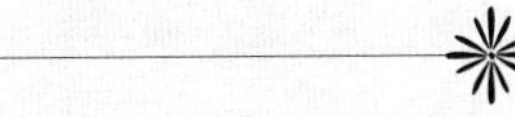

KEY PRAYER:

Lord, give me a love like Yours, an *agape* love for others that transcends the petty differences people have with one another. May love rule in my heart and life.

II CORINTHIANS

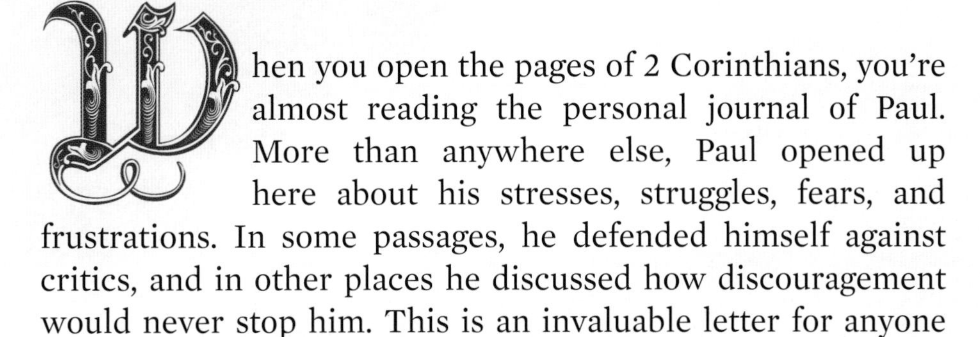

When you open the pages of 2 Corinthians, you're almost reading the personal journal of Paul. More than anywhere else, Paul opened up here about his stresses, struggles, fears, and frustrations. In some passages, he defended himself against critics, and in other places he discussed how discouragement would never stop him. This is an invaluable letter for anyone who feels under siege while in the Lord's work.

That doesn't mean 2 Corinthians is sad and defeatist. Rather, here we learn how Paul dealt with times when he was "troubled on every side. Outside were conflicts, inside were fears" (2 Corinthians 7:5). He trained himself "not [to] lose heart. Even though our outward man is perishing, yet the inward man is being renewed day by day.... While we do not look at the things which are seen, but at the things which are not seen" (4:16-18).

The secret to daily renewal is seeing those things that are

unseen. We have to focus our thoughts on God, who is invisible to us; on Christ, who is unseen by us at the moment; on the angelic forces around us; on our eternal home. We also have to take God's promises as given, trusting Him to bring about His visible results in His own timing, even if we see little visible progress at the moment.

When you're overwhelmed with life, remember that Paul sometimes felt the same. Yet he would not give up and he did not lose heart.

Neither should you!

KEY THEME:

Stresses and struggles in the work of Christ are real but temporary; service in the cause of Christ is glorious and eternal.

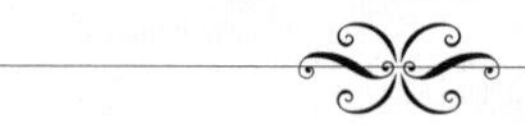

KEY CHALLENGE:

When overwhelmed, change your focus from the seen to the unseen.

KEY VERSE:

"For our light affliction, which is but for a moment, is working for us a far more exceeding and eternal weight of glory" (2 Corinthians 4:17).

KEY PRAYER:

Father, when I encounter obstacles and difficulties in serving You, help me to remember that service for You has eternal value.

GALATIANS

he New Testament letters were written to first-century churches, telling them how the Christian life was to be experienced. These new believers didn't yet have the New Testament, Bible colleges, seminaries, or generations of Christians as examples to follow.

Some got it wrong. After Paul had evangelized the Galatian region, some of his new converts were influenced by false teachers. In his letter to the Galatians, Paul wanted to correct mistaken beliefs and teach these churches about the true spiritual life.

In the first two chapters, Paul discussed the origin of the Gospel; and in the next two he reaffirmed its theology. The last two chapters explain the life of walking in the Spirit.

Galatians 5:16 says, "Walk in the Spirit, and you shall not fulfill the lust of the flesh." Within us are unhealthy desires and lusts.

We're tempted as we are drawn away by our own desires and enticed, which leads to sin (see James 1:14-15).

How do we overcome these tendencies?

The verse does *not* say: "Don't fulfill the lust of the flesh and you will walk in the Spirit." That thinking leads to legalism and defeat. We can't live victoriously in our own energy.

We are to walk in the Spirit, which means yielding ourselves continually and totally to Jesus, letting His Spirit rule our hearts in everything. When this is true, He will enable us to withstand the desires of the flesh.

To follow His orders, we must get things in the right order.

KEY THEME:

Discover God's sufficiency as you walk in the Spirit and not in the flesh.

KEY CHALLENGE:

If you're aware of an area in your life that is outside the control of the Holy Spirit, don't rest until you have fully yielded that area to Jesus.

KEY VERSE:

"I say then: Walk in the Spirit, and you shall not fulfill the lust of the flesh" (Galatians 5:16).

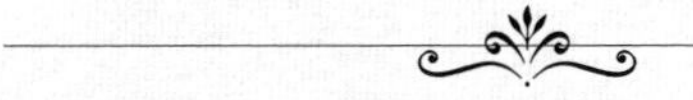

KEY PRAYER:

Lord, help me resist the desires of my flesh and choose instead to walk in Your Spirit today.

EPHESIANS

ow rich you are! The book of Ephesians describes the spiritual blessings that are ours in life and eternity. No book in the Bible makes us feel wealthier than Ephesians. Here God describes the inheritance He has prepared for those on whom His grace has been richly lavished.

In light of our wealth, we should live like spiritually rich people. The last half of Ephesians tells us how to do that. Paul began this section by saying, “I, therefore, the prisoner of the Lord, beseech you to walk worthy of the calling with which you were called” (Ephesians 4:1). In other words, since we are called to a life of wealth and privilege, we need to live in a way that reflects our high status in Christ.

That requires no longer walking as the Gentiles do, “in the futility of their mind” (4:17), but walking “in love, as Christ also has loved us” (5:2). We’re to walk as “children of light” (5:8), and we're to be "filled with the Spirit, speaking to one another in psalms and hymns and spiritual songs...giving thanks always... submitting to one another in the fear of God" (5:18-21).

Most of us don't feel very rich, and earthly riches don't satisfy us very long. But blessed be the God and Father of our Lord Jesus Christ! He has blessed us with every—not some, but every—spiritual blessing in the heavenly places in Christ.

Let's live a privileged life, like children of the King!

KEY THEME:

Enjoy peace with God and others and walk in love.

KEY CHALLENGE:

Thank God for your physical blessings but also thank Him for the spiritual blessings you have in Christ.

KEY VERSE:

"Blessed be the God and Father of our Lord Jesus Christ, who has blessed us with every spiritual blessing in the heavenly places in Christ" (Ephesians 1:3).

KEY PRAYER:

Lord, fill me with Your Spirit and empower me to love those around me with a love that comes from You.

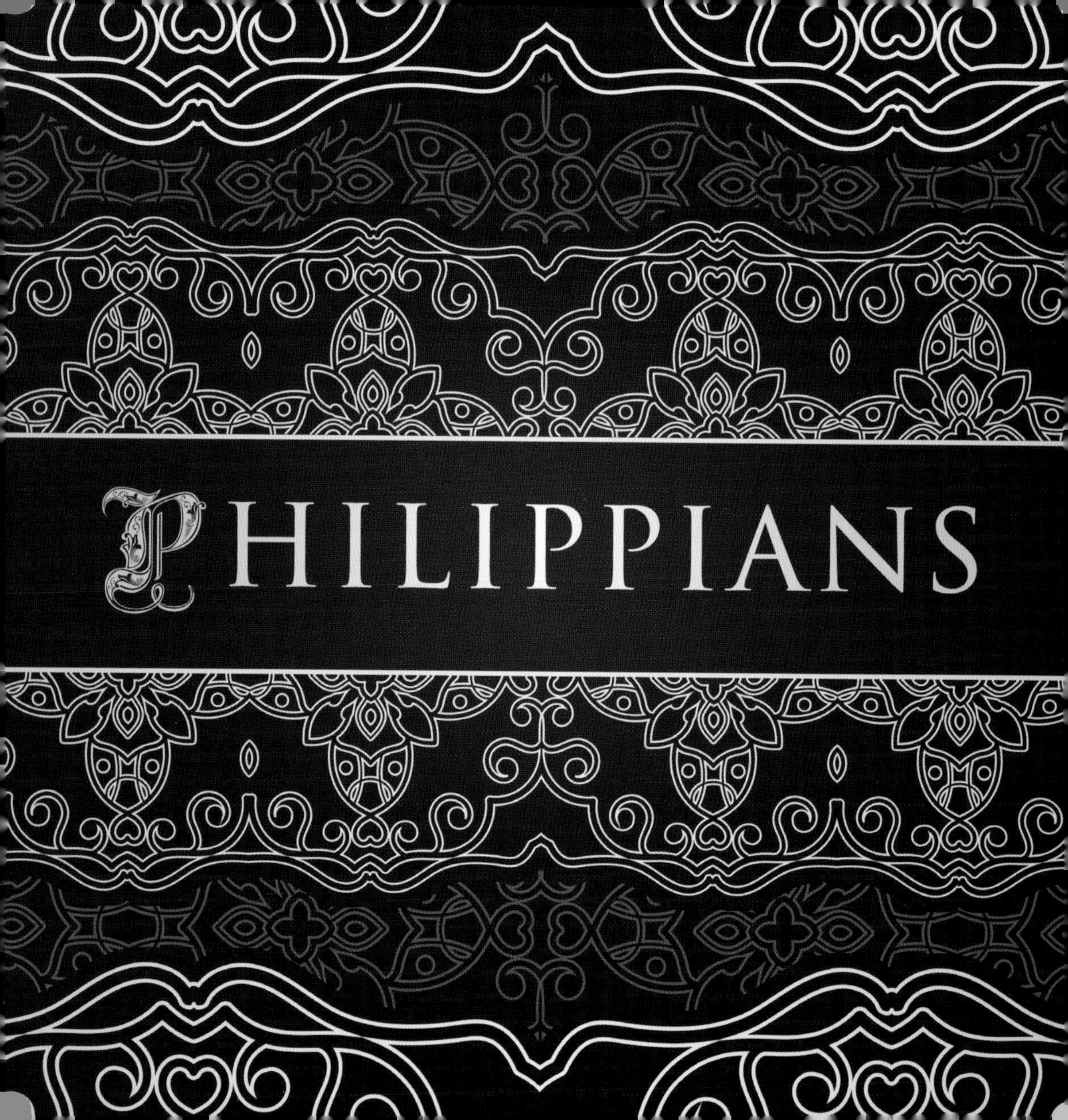
PHILIPPIANS

hilippians is one of the best books in the Bible for giving yourself an uplift in spirit. Though he was writing from prison, Paul filled this letter with expressions of joy and rejoicing, telling us to "rejoice in the Lord" (Philippians 3:1; 4:4). He also gave us an unbeatable motto for life: "For to me, to live is Christ, and to die is gain" (1:21).

Here in Philippians, we're pushed in a forward direction when it comes to our goals. Paul wrote, "But one thing I do, forgetting those things which are behind and reaching forward to those things which are ahead, I press toward the goal" (3:13-14).

In the last chapter, Paul outlined his method for overcoming worry, saying, "The Lord is at hand. Be anxious for nothing, but in everything by prayer and supplication, with thanksgiving, let your requests be made known to God" (4:5-6).

In the heart of the book, Paul wrote a song or poem about the humility of Christ, who left the highest throne in heaven to descend to earth as a Man to die for our sins. Few passages describe Jesus Christ using terms so lofty, yet so humble. Paul's purpose was to compel us to live humbly toward one another. If Jesus, being God, could humble Himself and become obedient to death on the cross, should not His children esteem others better than themselves and do all things without grumbling and disputing?

When you feel like grumbling, take a few minutes and dip into Philippians.

KEY THEME:

Don't be anxious. Walk in love, showing Christ's love and trusting in God's provision.

KEY CHALLENGE:

Put aside the burdens and cares of the past and press toward the future that God has prepared for you.

KEY VERSE:

"For to me, to live is Christ, and to die is gain" (Philippians 1:21).

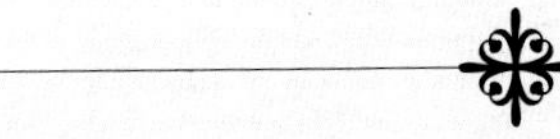

KEY PRAYER:

Father, thank You for Your Son's example of humility. May I exhibit the same humble mindset as Christ did while He was here on earth.

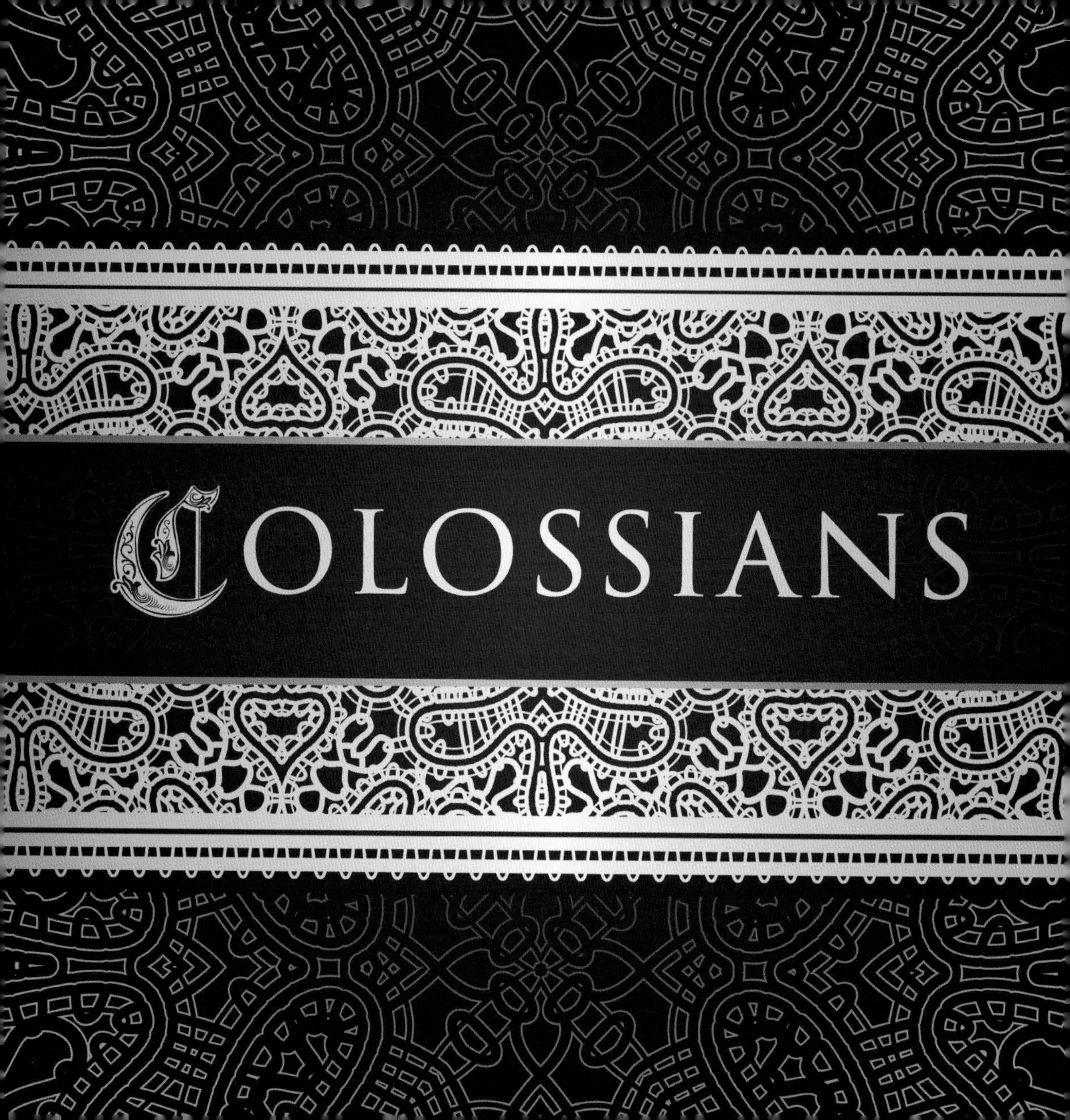
COLOSSIANS

henever you're being pulled down, look up. Set your mind on the risen, enthroned Christ, who is in all, through all, and over all. That's the message reverberating through Colossians.

The church in Colossae had been started by Epaphras, one of Paul's converts, who was concerned because false teachers were gaining a toehold among his members. When Epaphras asked Paul to write to the church, the apostle took the occasion to clarify and magnify the doctrine of the Person of Christ. Every false teaching distorts the doctrine of Christ in some way. Paul addressed that here, calling Jesus "the image of the invisible God" (Colossians 1:15).

Though we were dead in our sins, we have been raised to life in Him and through Him (2:13).

Since you have been raised with Christ, you should "seek those things which are above, where Christ is, sitting at the right hand of God. Set your mind on things above, not on things on the earth" (3:1-2).

We do that by meditating on Scripture. Many believers have experienced going for long walks or pacing around their houses during periods of discouragement, quoting Scripture and singing hymns of praise, deliberately shifting their thoughts and emotions upward toward the throne of God. It takes effort to lift our eyes to heaven. We have to dispense with self-pity and toxic anxiety and refocus on Him. The things of earth grow "strangely dim" when we seek the things above.

KEY THEME:

Since we have been raised with Christ, we must set our hearts on things above where Christ reigns, and we must do everything "heartily, as to the Lord" (Colossians 3:23).

KEY CHALLENGE:

Claim the truth of Christ and the power of the Holy Spirit by encouraging yourself in the Lord.

KEY VERSE:

"If then you were raised with Christ, seek those things which are above, where Christ is, sitting at the right hand of God" (Colossians 3:1).

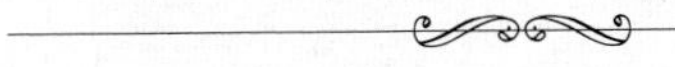

KEY PRAYER:

Lord, help me not to set my heart and mind on things here on earth, but to keep my focus on things above with You.

I THESSALONIANS

"or the Lord Himself will descend from heaven with a shout" (1 Thessalonians 4:16). When we really visualize that moment, it makes us want to shout too!

After Paul established a church in Thessalonica in Acts 17, he was driven from the area before he could give the new believers the extended teaching they needed. For example, he told them Christ would soon return, but he wasn't able to provide details. He wrote this letter to them, and every chapter ends with a reference to the Lord's return. Chapter 4 gives us the most vivid picture in the Bible of the moment when Christ will come in the air to Rapture His Church and raise those who have died in Him.

What encouragement! We're not to "sorrow as others who have no hope" (4:13). Instead, we're to "comfort one another with these words" (4:18).

But that's not all. The anticipation of our Lord's return should make us diligent soldiers, clad in the "breastplate of faith and love;" with the "hope of salvation" as our helmet (5:8). In this way, we'll be able to warn the unruly, comfort the fainthearted, uphold the weak, and be patient with everyone (5:14).

The biblical truths about the return of Christ aren't given simply to reveal our future. They are meant to enhance the quality of our present daily lives. Because Christ is coming for me one day, I must live in productive anticipation of His return—busy, hopeful, watchful—occupying my time wisely until He returns.

KEY THEME:

Since Christ may come at any moment, live productively, faithfully, and expectantly.

KEY CHALLENGE:

Live each day in expectation of the Lord's return!

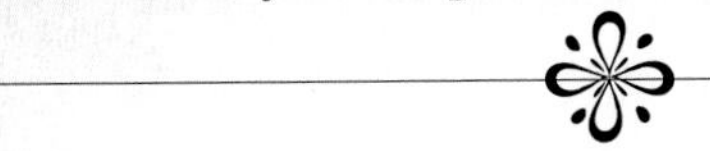

KEY VERSE:

"Therefore let us not sleep, as others do, but let us watch and be sober" (1 Thessalonians 5:6).

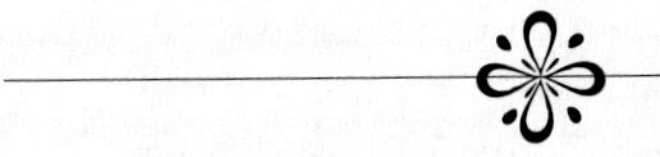

KEY PRAYER:

Heavenly Father, thank You for the imminent return of Christ for His Bride. May I live in productive anticipation as I await His return!

II THESSALONIANS

he more we learn about the return of Christ, the more we want to learn—and the harder we want to work for His cause! When Paul wrote 1 Thessalonians about the return of Christ, it simply whetted the Thessalonians' appetite to know more. So Paul wrote another letter with prophetic information that is essential for understanding the Second Coming. There are only three chapters in this small book. The first talks about the coming Day of the Lord. The second describes the rise and reign of the Antichrist, the "lawless one" (2 Thessalonians 2:9). And the third chapter tells us to be prayerful and industrious as we await our Lord's coming.

"But as for you, brethren," Paul wrote, "do not grow weary in doing good" (3:13).

A minister of past years once said he grew tired *in* the work, but not *of* the work, and that's what the apostle means here. As we go about the work before us each day, we often feel our energy drain away. Even our Lord became fatigued; He even fell asleep on a boat heading into a storm (Matthew 8:24). But He never became tired of the work assigned to Him.

God wants us to live enthusiastically, relishing the opportunities He gives us and trusting Him with the burdens we encounter. Our spirits should stay fresh. Our encouragement should be contagious. Get the rest you need and don't burn yourself out. But don't rust out either!

Keep doing good, and we will reap a harvest if we faint not (Galatians 6:9).

KEY THEME:

The Lord's return shouldn't provoke idleness among believers, but action; not speculation, but sanctification.

KEY CHALLENGE:

Don’t quit the work God has given you to do! Take time to rest and then ask Him for His strength to continue the work He has called you to.

KEY VERSE:

“But as for you, brethren, do not grow weary in doing good” (2 Thessalonians 3:13).

KEY PRAYER:

Lord, help me to keep focused on Your return and to live a godly life as I await that Day.

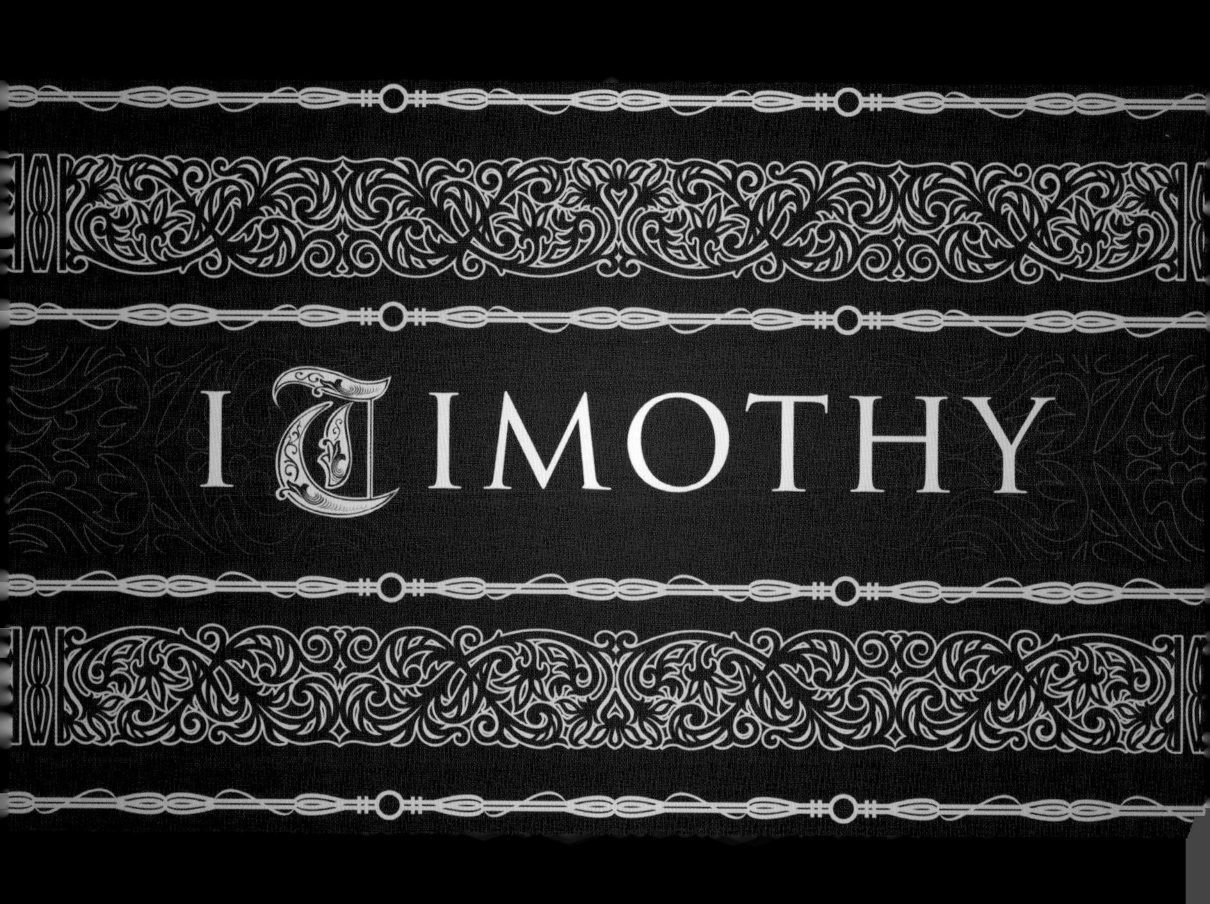
I TIMOTHY

esearchers tell us church attendance is dropping in the West, but the Bible says our Lord's Church is alive, well, vital, and growing. The world has been writing obituary notices for the Church for two thousand years. Yet in every generation, God has raised up godly pastors and leaders who will do as Paul told Timothy: "Be strong in the grace that is in Christ Jesus" (2 Timothy 2:1).

The books of 1 Timothy, 2 Timothy, and Titus are called Pastoral Epistles because they were written to men who headed up the work of local churches. Timothy oversaw the work in the city of Ephesus, and Titus worked on the island of Crete.

In 1 Timothy, Paul gave critical instructions for the management of the Church, including how to fight for the Gospel in a hostile culture (1 Timothy 1:3-20); the roles of prayer and of women (chapter 2); the process of finding leaders (chapter 3); what to do with those who fall away (chapter 4); and how to deal with various groups within the congregation (chapter 5). The final chapter is full of closing exhortations.

All of this tells us: The health of a local church is of utmost importance for His Kingdom. And no congregation is healthier than its individual members. Each of us must "be an example to the believers in word, in conduct, in love, in spirit, in faith, in purity," not neglecting our gifts, but continuing in them (1 Timothy 4:12-16).

Serve faithfully in your church and be an example to the other believers.

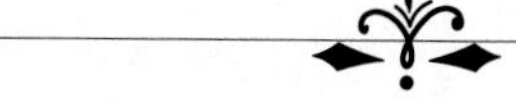

KEY THEME:

We must live holy lives that are pleasing to the Lord and devoted to the truth of His Word.

KEY CHALLENGE:

Be an encourager! Look for opportunities to uplift and bless others!

KEY VERSE:

"Let no one despise your youth, but be an example to the believers in word, in conduct, in love, in spirit, in faith, in purity" (1 Timothy 4:12).

KEY PRAYER:

Father, grant me wisdom and a servant's heart as I faithfully serve You in my local church.

II TIMOTHY

magine receiving a personal letter from a prisoner on death row, written just before his execution. That's what you're reading in 2 Timothy. This is Paul's final letter, addressed to his associate, Timothy—and to all of us—shortly before his execution in the days of Emperor Nero. If you read it against that background, you'll feel its emotional pull and finality. This was Paul's good-bye to us.

Two themes dominate the letter. The first half of the book (2 Timothy 1:1–2:13) encourages us to be strong, to fan into flame the gifts God has given us, and to never be ashamed of the Gospel. The last part of the letter (2:14–4:22) exhorts us to guard our ministry and our message, handling God's Word correctly and preaching the Word in season and out.

One special verse has guided church discipleship programs for centuries: "And the things that you have heard from me among many witnesses, commit these to faithful men who will be able to teach others also" (2:2). Notice the three generations here. Paul taught Timothy; Timothy taught faithful men; and these faithful men were to teach others.

Discipleship spreads from person to person, generation to generation. The process can be as simple as showing the younger members of your family how you go about your daily Bible study or quiet time. Discipling someone can be as informal as sharing verses of Scripture or as formal as a church discipleship group.

However it works for you, pass on to others what has been passed on to you.

KEY THEME:

Disciple those who are younger in the faith so they will be able to disciple others also.

KEY CHALLENGE:

Whatever your age, make yourself available to share and teach the Word to others!

KEY VERSE:

"You therefore, my son, be strong in the grace that is in Christ Jesus. And the things that you have heard from me among many witnesses, commit these to faithful men who will be able to teach others also" (2 Timothy 2:1-2).

KEY PRAYER:

Lord, thank You for those who have discipled me in my faith. Now please give me opportunities to disciple others as well.

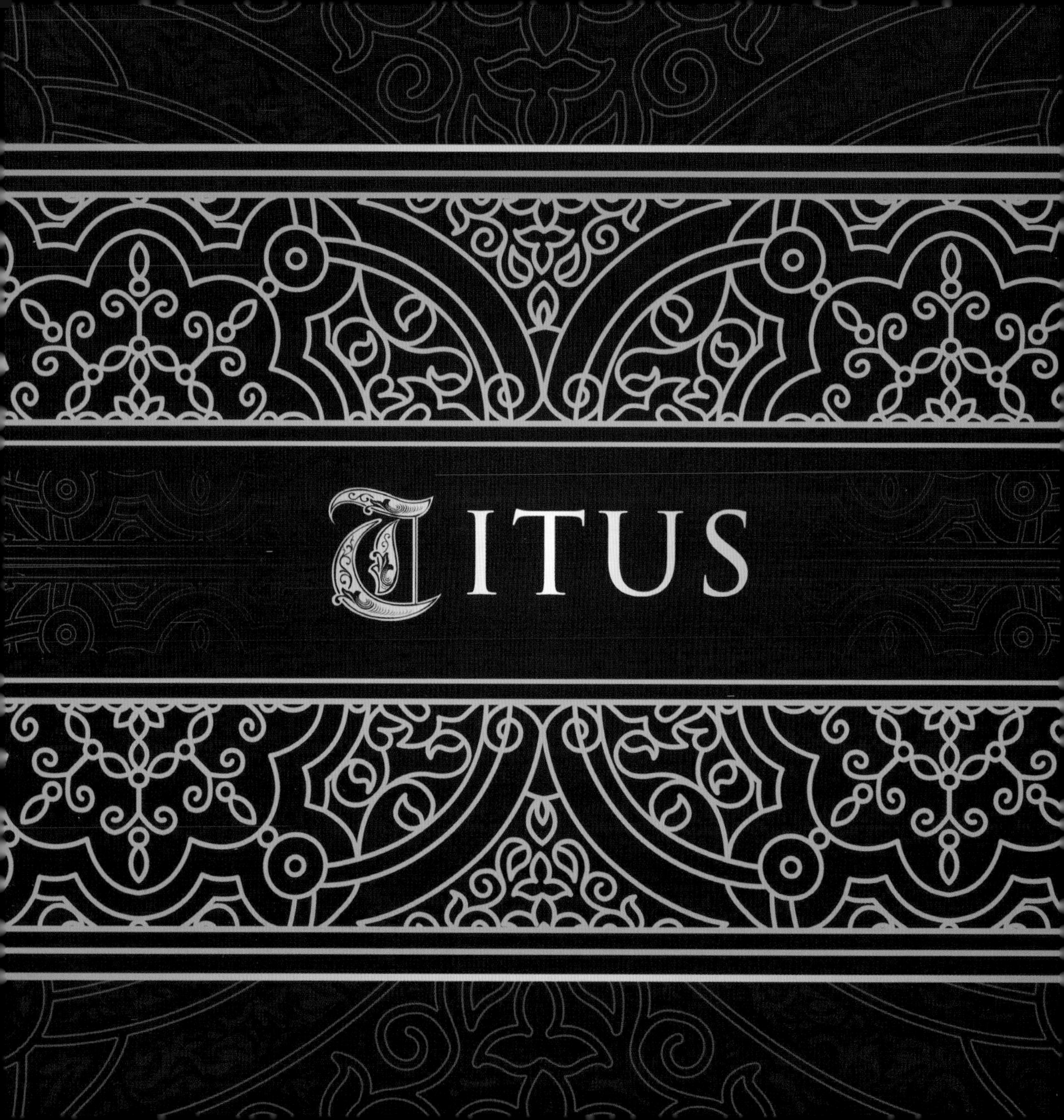
TITUS

itus is the book to read when you're sick and tired of the culture. It's easy to grow weary in a world of indecent entertainment, four-letter words, laziness, indulgence, violence, and godless philosophies. That's a perfect description for the island of Crete in the first century. Paul and Titus toured the island, preaching the Gospel and starting fledging churches. When Paul sailed away, he left Titus there to "set in order the things that are lacking" (Titus 1:5).

That included biblical teaching. We can't reform the culture without reclaiming individuals, and that can't happen without sound doctrine. Paul stressed to Titus the need to teach new Christians theology and to censure false teachers.

Our behavior flows from our beliefs. What we say and do is determined by what we think. Before applying the truth, we need to know the truth. That's why taking a verse out of context doesn't build deep churches or solid Christians. It's easy in a sermon or lesson to take a miscellaneous verse, add a story, and make some application. But unless the truth is presented in context and with adequate background, it's of limited use.

Shallow insights create hollow saints. Whenever you have an opportunity to write, speak, teach, or preach from God's Word, do so studiously and seriously. Unfold the Scripture, make the application, and ask God to change a soul—and a society.

Let's hold fast the faithful word that we may be able, by sound doctrine, to exhort and convict the world (1:9).

KEY THEME:

Teach sound doctrine and live a godly life.

KEY CHALLENGE:

Stay grounded in the Word of God and trust in its promises—it will be your firm foundation in a world filled with uncertainty and disbelief.

KEY VERSE:

"But as for you, speak the things which are proper for sound doctrine" (Titus 2:1).

KEY PRAYER:

Lord, my desire is to be a diligent student of Your Word and to share it with others as they begin their walk of faith. I pray that You will help me be a faithful witness for Your glory and honor.

PHILEMON

he final Pauline letter in the New Testament is a short, personal note to a man named Philemon, who lived in the city of Colossae. From details in the letter, we can piece together the story that led to its writing. In the Roman world, slavery was pervasive and part of the cultural worldview. Philemon's young slave, Onesimus, stole some money and ran away. The young fugitive had apparently come to his wits' end in Rome and had sought out Paul, who was under house arrest there. Paul led him to Christ and sent him back with this note, telling Philemon to receive Onesimus back, not as a slave, but as a brother.

This little book has been one of history's greatest anti-slavery documents, but it also stands out as a treatise on forgiveness and reconciliation. This simple letter not only answered any questions Philemon had about where Onesimus was, it let him know that he was a changed man. In an everyday sense, it also teaches us the art of uplifting others. Paul encouraged Philemon with his letter, and the apostle also told him: "the hearts of the saints have been refreshed by you, brother" (Philemon 1:7). And Paul asked him, "refresh my heart in the Lord" (verse 20).

With the right frame of mind and loving positive attitude, you can be a source of inspiration and encouragement for someone today!

KEY THEME:

Receive, respect, and refresh your brothers and sisters in Christ.

KEY CHALLENGE:

Look for opportunities to spiritually encourage and refresh others—give them the gift of encouragement.

KEY VERSE:

"For we have great joy and consolation in your love, because the hearts of the saints have been refreshed by you, brother" (Philemon 1:7).

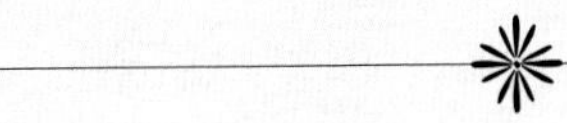

KEY PRAYER:

Father, I pray that I will be a source of encouragement and blessing for my brothers and sisters in Christ by my life, my words, and my actions.

HEBREWS

ven seasoned, veteran Christians can feel overwhelmed and grow discouraged by life's relentless troubles. An unknown writer (Luke? Apollos? Barnabas?) grew concerned about some Hebrew Christians in the first century. Years before they had started their Christian experience amid persecution but with great enthusiasm (Hebrews 10:32-34). Now they were facing renewed pressure and were in danger of reverting to their old faith. Could some of them relapse back into a Christless Judaism (10:35)?

In this letter, our author insists that Jesus is greater than anything in the Old Testament. He is superior to the prophets (1:1-2), the angels (1:4), the law of Moses (7:19), and the priesthood of Aaron (7:11-17). He Himself is our great High Priest (4:14) and the atoning sacrifice for our sins (10:12). He will never leave us or forsake us (13:5), and He knows exactly what we are going through (2:18).

One great exhortation runs all the way through Hebrews—persevere! Don't give up and don't quit. "Let us lay aside every weight, and the sin which so easily ensnares us, and let us run with endurance the race that is set before us, looking unto Jesus" (Hebrews 12:1-2).

"You have need of endurance, so that after you have done the will of God, you may receive the promise" (Hebrews 10:36).

Times are tough, but that's when we need to turn to this wonderful book. Every verse in Hebrews is ammunition against discouragement. Whatever your lot today, hold fast to the "confession of [your] hope without wavering, for He who promised is faithful" (Hebrews 10:23).

KEY THEME:

Persevere in your faith and discipleship.

KEY CHALLENGE:

Prepare for the race ahead so that you will endure and finish strong in your faith, leaving a legacy for others to follow.

KEY VERSE:

"Let us hold fast the confession of our hope without wavering, for He who promised is faithful" (Hebrews 10:23).

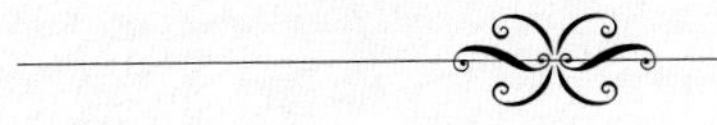

KEY PRAYER:

God, help me to hold fast to Your promises and to persevere as I await Christ's return.

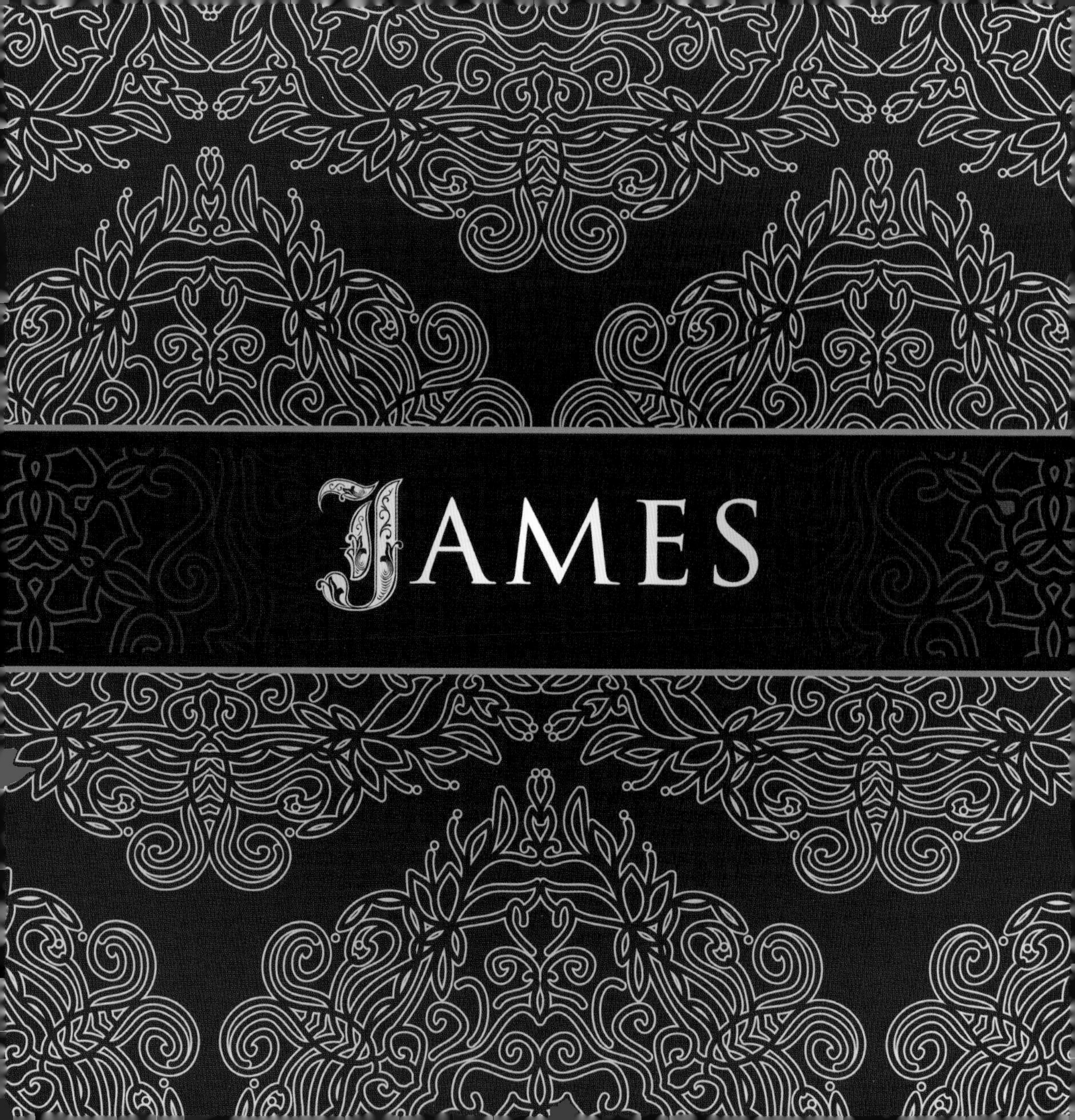
JAMES

an you imagine what would it have been like to have grown up in the tiny village of Nazareth as part of the holy family? Your mother—Mary. Your father—Joseph. Your big brother—Jesus. Imagine these five brothers all sharing the same little bedroom—Jesus, James, Joses, Simon, and Judas (also known as Jude) (Matthew 13:55).

That actually happened to two of the New Testament authors. Near the end of the Bible we come to the books of James and Jude, both attributed to men who had grown up with Jesus Himself.

James bends over backward not to leverage his unique place. He refers to himself only as "a bondservant of God and of the Lord Jesus Christ" (James 1:1). Only once more does He mention the Lord's name, in chapter 2, when he speaks of "the faith of our Lord Jesus Christ, the Lord of glory" (verse 1). Instead of talking *about* Jesus, he talked *like* Jesus. Many people have compared James' letter to the Sermon on the Mount. When we read the book of James, it sounds just like we are listening to the teachings of Jesus.

That's why James is such a practical, down-to-earth book, telling us how to be doers of the Word (1:22), putting action to our faith and living out our Christian testimony (2:17). He stresses the way we control our temper (1:19-20) and control our tongue (3:1-12). He wants our words to be truthful (5:12).

Implementing James is as simple as doing a good deed today. Let someone see Jesus in your attitude and actions before the sun goes down!

KEY THEME:

True faith demands a committed life where we care for widows and orphans and pursue personal holiness.

KEY CHALLENGE:

Determine to put your faith into action and make your life a reflection of Jesus by blessing others in His Name.

KEY VERSE:

"Pure and undefiled religion before God and the Father is this: to visit orphans and widows in their trouble, and to keep oneself unspotted from the world" (James 1:27).

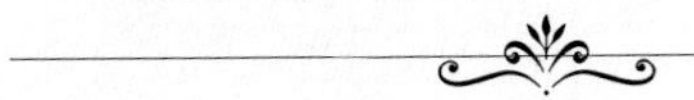

KEY PRAYER:

Lord, help me live a life that reflects Your love by helping widows, orphans, and other needy souls around me.

I PETER

eter couldn't be everywhere at once. He longed to be in every congregation as persecution rolled across Asia Minor. Unable to do so, he wrote a letter "to the pilgrims of the Dispersion in Pontus, Galatia, Cappadocia, Asia, and Bithynia"—and to us (1 Peter 1:1). His theme was to show how Jesus provided a model for endurance in suffering: "For to this you were called, because Christ also suffered for us, leaving us an example, that you should follow His steps" (2:21).

But Peter knew the Christian experience is more than endurance. It's evangelism, using every situation to share the Good News. In chapter 3, he gave us a four-fold strategy for reaching others. We must (1) sanctify the Lord in our hearts, fully committed to Him and to His Word and His ways; (2) cultivate such a hopeful attitude that others will notice; (3) be ready to share the reason for that hope; and to (4) do so with a gentle, positive attitude.

All this is found in one of the Bible's greatest verses on apologetics and evangelism—1 Peter 3:15.

Let's do just as Peter said! Start by giving yourself anew to the Lord. Set apart your life for Him, asking Him for a fresh anointing. Change the attitude of your heart and the appearance of your face to reflect your thrilling certainty of eternal life. Prepare what you'll say when someone asks about your hope. And follow up with gentle enthusiasm.

That's the greatest evangelistic method ever known.

KEY THEME:

We should always be prepared to defend our faith when someone asks us about the hope we have in Christ.

KEY CHALLENGE:

Ask the Lord to send someone your way who needs the hope of the Gospel and be ready to share your faith unashamedly with them.

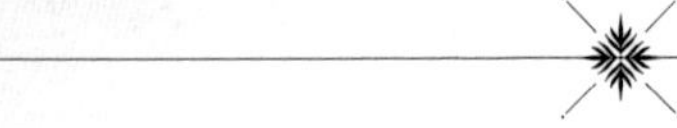

KEY VERSE:

"But sanctify the Lord God in your hearts, and always be ready to give a defense to everyone who asks you a reason for the hope that is in you, with meekness and fear" (1 Peter 3:15).

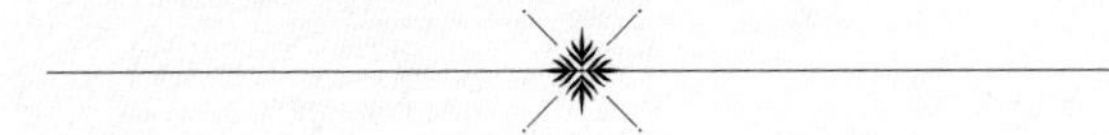

KEY PRAYER:

Lord, please give me the right words to speak when someone asks me about the hope I have in You. My desire is to share Your love with others.

II PETER

If 2 Timothy represents the last words of Paul, 2 Peter does the same for the apostle Peter, one of the Lord's original disciples. He, too, was executed in Rome during the reign of Nero. That makes his words all the more precious. His chapters deal with three final issues he wanted to emphasize. Chapter 1 is devoted to the vitality of our individual faith. He wanted us to "be even more diligent" to grow in Christ (2 Peter 1:10). His second chapter sounds a lot like the book of Jude. It's a warning against heretics. His final chapter looks forward to the return of Christ, a subject never far from his thoughts.

It should never be far from ours either.

Students of biblical prophecy view 2 Peter 3 as crucial to our understanding of the events related to the Second Coming. But more than that, Peter wants us to live today in light of tomorrow's promises.

"Therefore, since all these things will be dissolved, what manner of persons ought you to be in holy conduct and godliness.... Therefore, beloved, looking forward to these things, be diligent to be found by Him in peace, without spot" (3:11, 14).

Think of our Lord's return often, but don't just relegate it to a future event. Consider its immediate implications. If you had important guests coming tomorrow, what would you do to prepare for them now?

Let's live as those who expect our Lord to come tomorrow—or today!

KEY THEME:

Anticipate the Lord's coming and live peaceably with those around you until then.

KEY CHALLENGE:

Live with expectation of Christ's return but also treasure today as you share your faith with those who are lost.

KEY VERSE:

"Therefore, beloved, looking forward to these things, be diligent to be found by Him in peace, without spot and blameless" (2 Peter 3:14).

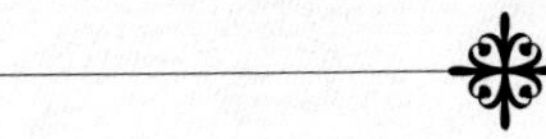

KEY PRAYER:

Father, help me to live a peaceable life as I eagerly wait for the Rapture of the Church.

I JOHN

e're never too old to do what the Lord ordains every day. The apostle John, last of the original disciples, was elderly, but he was as diligent as ever in watching over the house churches of Ephesus and of Asia Minor. He wrote the Fourth Gospel in old age, then he reinforced it in this circular letter to his churches.

John had lived long enough to know two things. First, God loved us enough to send His Son to die for us. That's John 3:16. In the parallel verse of 1 John 3:16, John took it a step further. We should love others enough to give our lives for them, whether by dying or by living for them.

John was concerned about disunity in his churches, churches that were also being threatened by false teachers (1 John 2:18). So he stressed the need to keep doctrine pure and love strong. Those were his two great themes in this letter.

And what is love? It's the quality of spotting a need in someone's life and meeting it. "But whoever has this world's goods," he wrote, "and sees his brother in need, and shuts up his heart from him, how does the love of God abide in him?" (3:17)

John's definition of love is a reversal of the world's view, which says, "Come, meet my need!" As we grow in Christ, He gives us special eyesight to spot those with needs—physical, material, emotional, relational, or spiritual. He also provides insight into meeting the need.

Special eyesight to see. Special insight to act. That is biblical love!

KEY THEME:

He laid down His life for us, and we also ought to lay down our lives—and take them up—for our brothers and sisters.

KEY CHALLENGE:

Look for someone who has a need, great or small, that you can help in Jesus' Name.

KEY VERSE:

"By this we know love, because He laid down His life for us. And we also ought to lay down our lives for the brethren" (1 John 3:16).

KEY PRAYER:

Heavenly Father, thank You for the gift of Your Son. May I love others with the love of Christ—sacrificially and unconditionally.

II JOHN

he Bible's straightforward message is anchored in historical events. Events like the call of Abraham to Canaan; the possessing of the Promised Land under Joshua; the anointing of David as King over Israel; the birth of Jesus, and His death and resurrection; and the events surrounding the Day of Pentecost.

The book of Romans and the other epistles help us understand the significance of these events by giving us doctrine, which reveals God's intentions in the things He has done.

As we carefully and correctly study the Bible, the major themes become clear. We see both His works and His words.

Still, there is no end to deceivers who come with false messages, twisting the Scriptures and presenting a counterfeit message. John wrote all three of his letters to counter heretics. In the tiny book of 2 John, he wrote to one church (the elect lady and her children), reminding them to love each other (2 John 1:4-6), but exhorting them to guard against the "many deceivers" who "have gone out into the world [and] do not confess Jesus Christ as coming in the flesh" (2 John 1:7).

Just as one ink spot on a clean tablecloth attracts all our attention, so the blot of false teaching ruins a church or a Christian life.

This is why we study the Bible so carefully, choose our teachers with discretion, and study the subject of doctrine and theology. Some people groan at the thought of doctrine, but the truths of theology make sense of what God has done in history—and for us, that is thrilling!

KEY THEME:

If we're vigilant against deceivers and deception,
we'll receive a full reward without losing
the things we've worked for.

KEY CHALLENGE:

Prepare yourself for the false messages that the world offers by being a student of the Truth. Be an unapologetic voice for the unchanging Word of God in your circle of friends and family.

KEY VERSE:

"Look to yourselves, that we do not lose those things we worked for, but that we may receive a full reward" (2 John 1:8).

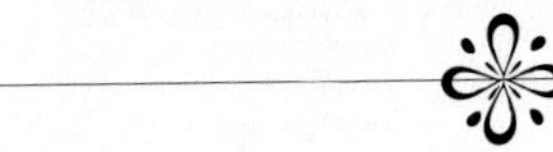

KEY PRAYER:

Lord, give me discernment against false teaching and deception and a diligent pursuit of Truth that will help me illumine the lives of others.

III JOHN

hank God for good Bible teachers! We are blessed by those who diligently study the Word, gain fresh insights and applications, then preach, teach, and write for our benefit!

From the beginning of the Church, the Lord has raised up teachers. In New Testament days, many of these teachers traveled on primitive roads, making their way through dangerous areas, and showing up in towns and villages to teach believers. That pattern has gone on for two thousand years. God's people have always needed hospitable people to welcome them.

Today we have restaurants, airplanes, hotels, and an entire hospitality industry. But there's still a role for us to play in offering an open door for those needing it. A man named Gaius did that in his hometown in Asia Minor, and John wrote this little letter thanking him. His home was always open to John and to the itinerate evangelists and teachers who traveled about.

The church in his town likely met in his home too.

Not a single house in biblical times had air conditioning, electricity, a gas range, or a hot shower. Yet they entertained so much more than most of us! Gone may be the days when we had guest rooms and prophet's chambers, but there is always a way to open our home, however humble, to others.

Prepare a meal. Make some cookies. Offer a refreshing drink to a delivery agent. Have a friend over for tea. Open your home for a Bible study.

Let's learn once again the biblical art of hospitality.

KEY THEME:

Diligently encourage God's work and show hospitality to His workers.

KEY CHALLENGE:

Make a plan to bless those who work in ministry—find opportunities to uphold, to help, and to encourage someone who has dedicated their life to the work of the Lord.

KEY VERSE:

"Beloved, you do faithfully whatever you do for the brethren and for strangers, who have borne witness of your love before the church. If you send them forward on their journey in a manner worthy of God, you will do well" (3 John 1:5-6).

KEY PRAYER:

Lord, provide me with opportunities to show hospitality to those who are serving You in ministry.

JUDE

Jude gives us two great commands: to "contend earnestly for the faith" (Jude 1:3), and to keep ourselves "in the love of God" (verse 21).

While most of Jude involves the first issue (verses 3-19), the writer ends with the second: "But you, beloved, building yourselves up on your most holy faith, praying in the Holy Spirit, keep yourselves in the love of God, looking for the mercy of our Lord Jesus Christ unto eternal life" (verses 20-21).

The main command here is to keep yourself in the love of God, which corresponds to our Lord's words in John 15: "Abide in Me, and I in you.... Abide in My love" (verses 4, 9). Jude wanted to remind us of the importance of abiding in Christ, remaining in Him, and keeping in His love. That is, we need to grow closer to our Lord each day. How do we do that?

First, by building ourselves up on our "most holy faith" (verse 20). To keep growing in our ability to trust God in all situations, finding His promises in times of distress by putting our full weight on them.

Second, by "praying in the Holy Spirit" (verse 20). Ask the Spirit to give you fervor and power in prayer.

Third, by looking forward to the "mercy of our Lord" when He comes (verse 21). Anticipate the mercy the Lord Jesus will bring when He ushers us into eternity.

Which of those three areas do you need to work on the most?

KEY THEME:

A call to remember! Contend earnestly for the faith, so that all wisdom, glory, and power will be unto our God and Savior.

KEY CHALLENGE:

Make it a commitment to put your faith into action—contend for it, embrace it, seek it, trust it—it is precious!

KEY VERSE:

"Beloved...I found it necessary to write to you exhorting you to contend earnestly for the faith which was once for all delivered to the saints" (Jude 1:3).

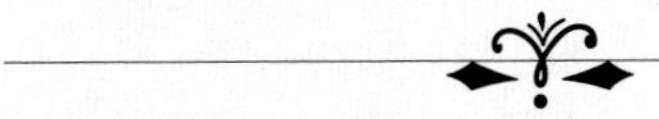

KEY PRAYER:

Father, help me to stand firm in my faith as I live for You in the world today.

REVELATION

hen it clicked! Have you ever had that experience? Something seemed baffling, intimidating, beyond your ability to figure it out. But as you kept studying, reading, and reviewing the matter, suddenly it clicked. You began to see how it all fit together.

That's how it is with Revelation.

This book is God's way of ending His Bible by making us think. He especially wants us to think about the upcoming future, the Rapture of the Church, the events of the Tribulation, the return of Christ, and our glorious eternal future in His new heavens, new earth, and New Jerusalem.

If you don't understand Revelation, keep reading it, studying it, and thinking through its pages. With the help of the Holy Spirit, it will start fitting together in a way that will thrill you with anticipation.

To encourage us to continue on, we have two promises from God. Revelation 1:3 says we are blessed by reading the book; and Revelation 22:7 says, "Behold, I am coming quickly! Blessed is he who keeps the words of the prophecy of this book."

The events of history are swirling together into a tornado that will lead directly to the return of Christ. Everything worthless and worldly will be swept away, but those who love Jesus will inherit all He has promised.

The last invitation of the Bible invites *whoever desires* to come and drink from the fountain of eternal life, which is Jesus Christ Himself. I urge you to do that today!

KEY THEME:

Christ is returning. Whoever desires is invited to come and to drink of the waters of eternal life, and live!

KEY CHALLENGE:

The end-time events have been revealed, the invitation to come has been offered, and now we need to do our part to share these truths with those who have not heard of this glorious salvation. The time is short, so make each moment count for Him.

KEY VERSE:

"Blessed is he who reads and those who hear the words of this prophecy, and keep those things which are written in it; for the time is near" (Revelation 1:3).

KEY PRAYER:

Heavenly Father, thank You for Your marvelous gift of salvation. All glory and praise be to the Lamb, my Savior and soon-coming King!

Additional Resources
FROM DR. DAVID JEREMIAH

The Jeremiah Study Bible

Drawing from more than forty years of study and teaching, Dr. David Jeremiah has compiled *The Jeremiah Study Bible*. This legacy resource is now available in three versions—the New King James, NIV, and ESV, in regular or large print options. This trusted resource was purposefully designed to allow the reader to understand: What It Says, What It Means, and What It Means for You.

This unique Study Bible features thousands of study notes, hundreds of enriching word studies, historical insights, more than 50 *Essentials of the Christian Faith* articles, nearly 100 maps, charts, and tables, with additional links to online resources.

The Jeremiah Study Bible is a wonderful resource for every student of the Bible—new convert, teacher, layman, or pastor.

ADDITIONAL RESOURCES

When Your World Falls Apart

When life suddenly turns upside down, there, in the midst of your trials and in the center of your pain, is God—comforting, guiding, encouraging, teaching, sustaining. In this perceptive and deeply personal book, Dr. David Jeremiah draws from the beautiful poetry and deep truths of the Psalms—passages that gave him comfort and strength on his journey into the unknown. Interwoven with his own reflections and insights are the inspiring real-life stories of other men and women who have faced unexpected adversity and found that God's grace is truly sufficient for every need.

Answers to Questions About Living in the Last Days

How are we to live as we wait for Christ's return? In this book, Dr. Jeremiah offers biblical insights into living with confidence and purpose as we wait for the coming of our Lord. This book provides answers to more than seventy questions that are weighing on the minds of Christians and non-Christians alike in these perilous times.

ADDITIONAL RESOURCES

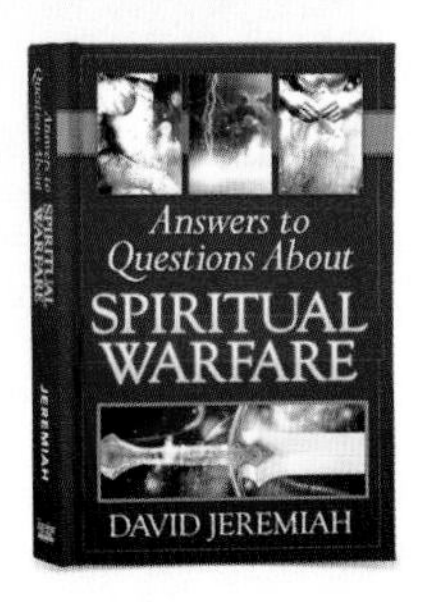

Answers to Questions About Spiritual Warfare

Troubling circumstances have a way of claiming our attention! But if we fail to view daily spiritual challenges against the big picture of spiritual warfare, we can draw wrong conclusions and implement ineffective strategies. In *Answers to Questions About Spiritual Warfare* you will find selected answers to every pertinent question concerning victory in the spiritual realm.

Answers to Questions About Adversity

Why, we wonder, is life so difficult? This question has haunted humanity from the beginning. The Bible has answers for us—not easy answers, but rich, satisfying, grace-tinted answers. But where in the Bible do we turn when perplexed? *Answers to Questions About Adversity* is an instant source of eternal help. How wonderful to know that God has answers to our questions!

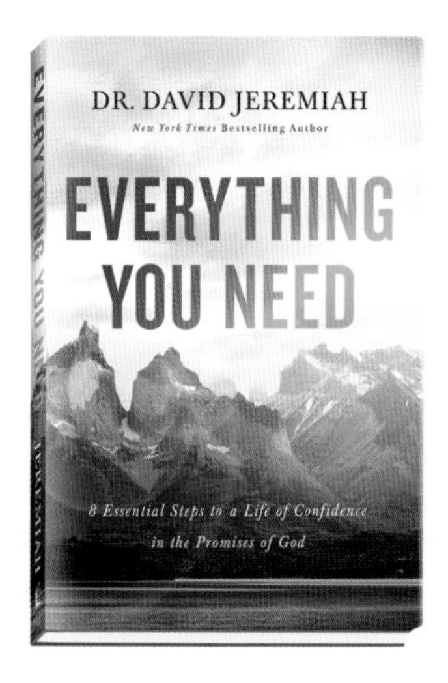

Everything You Need: 8 Essential Steps to a Life of Confidence in the Promises of God!

Have you ever seen so many people under so much pressure? That's the nature of our times, but don't despair! God has given you *everything you need* to withstand the stresses of life and overcome the challenges of the journey. According to the apostle Peter, God knows how to equip you for life and godliness. He has given you His very great and precious promises. Through them you can escape the corruption of the world and begin living with steadfast, daily confidence.

Near the end of his life when he was facing pressures of his own, Peter wrote one of the Bible's greatest descriptions of sure-footed living—2 Peter 1:3-9. As Dr. Jeremiah walks you through this passage, you'll discover how God's promises steady our steps and guide our pathways. As you immerse yourself in the unfolding logic of this passage, you'll gain a fresh understanding of God's power, His promises, and His purposes.

ADDITIONAL RESOURCES

Forward: Discovering God's Presence and Purpose in Your Tomorrow

Do you feel like your best days are behind you? It is time to quit looking in the rearview mirror and to focus on the road ahead of you. God is not finished with you! It doesn't matter who you are, or what your age or your current situation may be, God is ready to partner with you to fulfill your desires and His purpose for your life. In Forward, author and Bible teacher, David Jeremiah invites you to follow the apostle Paul in "forgetting those things which are behind and reaching forward to those things which are ahead" (Philippians 3:13).

Forward gives practical insights into "what's next" in your life, with a step-by-step action plan to move past where you are today to where you want to be. You'll discover how God wants to expand your dream, to give you divine direction, to help you understand your life purpose, to equip you with tools to overcome fear, to experience personal accomplishment through His leading, and to realize a mission and purpose that will outlive your life.